Abiding in Emptiness

Abiding in Emptiness

A Guide for Meditative Practice

Bhikkhu Anālayo

Wisdom

Wisdom Publications
132 Perry Street
New York, NY 10014 USA
wisdomexperience.org

Library of Congress Cataloging-in-Publication Data
Names: Anālayo, 1962– author.
Title: Abiding in emptiness: a guide for meditative practice / Bhikkhu Anālayo.
Description: First edition. | New York: Wisdom Publications, 2024. |
Includes bibliographical references and index.
Identifiers: LCCN 2023026348 (print) | LCCN 2023026349 (ebook) |
ISBN 9781614299172 (hardcover) | ISBN 9781614299325 (ebook)
Subjects: LCSH: Meditation—Buddhism. | Sunyata. | Buddhism—Doctrines.
Classification: LCC BQ5620 .A53 2024 (print) | LCC BQ5620 (ebook) |
DDC 296.7/2—dc23/eng/20230918
LC record available at https://lccn.loc.gov/2023026348
LC ebook record available at https://lccn.loc.gov/2023026349

ISBN 978-1-61429-917-2 ebook ISBN 978-1-61429-932-5

28 27 26 25 24
5 4 3 2 1

Cover design by Jess Morphew. Interior design by Tony Lulek. The index was not compiled by the author.

As an act of Dhammadāna, Bhikkhu Anālayo has waived royalty payments for this book.

Printed on acid-free paper that meets the guidelines for permanence and durability of the Production Guidelines for Book Longevity of the Council on Library Resources.

Printed in the United States of America.

Contents

Acknowledgments

I AM INDEBTED TO Chris Burke, Bhikkhunī Dhammadinnā, Linda Grace, Sarah Kirchberger, and Yuka Nakamura for commenting on a draft version of this book and to the staff, board members, and supporters of the Barre Center for Buddhist Studies for providing me with the facilities needed to do my practice and writing.

Introduction

THE FOLLOWING PAGES present a practice-related exploration of emptiness in daily life and formal meditation, based on instructions found in the Greater and the Smaller Discourses on Emptiness. My presentation proceeds through eight chapters, providing translations of the relevant textual portions followed by explanations, a summary of the main points covered in each chapter, and practice instructions.

My own practice of abiding in emptiness has greatly benefited from receiving teachings, some thirty years ago, from Chan Master Shengyi (a disciple of Master Xuyun) and from Tulku Urgyen Rinpoche. A profound shift in my practice happened in particular after receiving the pointing-out instructions from Tulku Urgyen Rinpoche. In addition, I recently had the honor and pleasure to teach emptiness practice together with Guogu (a disciple of Master Shengyan) and again with Yongey Mingyur Rinpoche (a son of Tulku Urgyen Rinpoche). As I write these lines, my heart fills with a deep sense of gratitude for what I was able to learn from each of these encounters.

The presentation in what follows is firmly grounded in early Buddhist thought. In other words, although my emptiness meditation practice is clearly influenced by my encounters with the above teachers, I have from the outset contextualized such practice within the doctrinal framework provided by the early discourses, in clear awareness that this differs in some respects from perspectives underlying the Chan and the Mahāmudrā/Dzogchen traditions.

Versions of the Greater and the Smaller Discourses on Emptiness exist in Pāli, Chinese, and Tibetan. Nevertheless, meditation on emptiness in its various forms has not garnered as much attention from Theravādins as it has from practitioners of Chinese and Tibetan Buddhism. In an attempt to build a bridge between these different traditions and to facilitate an adoption of emptiness practices by contemporary practitioners operating within the framework of Theravāda thought, I have based my translations entirely on Pāli discourse passages. At the same time, my hope is that this approach will also reveal to practitioners from other Buddhist traditions how much common ground can be found, thereby serving as a source of mutual appreciation and inspiration.

Although I base my presentation on the Pāli sources, in my annotations I nevertheless provide a comparative perspective on such quotations, and in the case of a clear transmission error in the Smaller Discourse on Emptiness I rely on the Chinese and Tibetan parallels to clarify the Pāli version. In this way, my approach is still based on early Buddhist source material, representing the earliest period of Buddhist thought still accessible today and the common heritage of all Buddhist traditions.[1] Out of the different sources available for reconstructing early Buddhist thought, in the present case I give primacy to the Pāli versions. This differs from my usual approach of translating the Chinese versions, mainly motivated by the fact that these have for the most part not yet been translated into English, whereas reliable translations of their Pāli counterparts are readily available.

In the case of the Greater and the Smaller Discourses on Emptiness, however, I already translated the Chinese versions as part of a study of *Compassion and Emptiness in Early Buddhist Meditation*.[2] In the final part of that study, I surveyed practical implementations of meditation on the "divine abodes" (*brahmavihāra*), alternatively also known as states that are "immeasurable" or "boundless" (Pāli: *appamāṇa*; Sanskrit: *apramāṇa*), and on emptiness. According to the feedback I received after publication, whereas the part on the divine abodes seemed to work, the instructions on emptiness meditation were apparently too terse and insufficient for guiding actual practice. This made it clear to me that there was a need to take up such practical application in more detail. In the meantime, I have also explored the significance of signlessness more fully. This forms part of an attempt to make sense of descriptions of Nirvana in early Buddhist texts from the viewpoint of the construction of experience, resulting in a study titled *The Signless and the Deathless: On the Realization of Nirvana.*[3] This study provides a more detailed background to the practices taken up in the final two chapters of my present exploration.

Regarding the meditation practices described in the following pages, particularly in the last chapters, I need to alert the reader to the fact that these can result in mental imbalance if wrongly undertaken. This holds particularly for someone with a trauma-related personal history.[4] For this reason, when personally teaching meditation, I try to ensure that practitioners have a firm grounding in embodied mindfulness and the divine abodes *before* embarking on emptiness meditation. Since I am here sharing the practices in book form, I can only alert to the overarching need to maintain balance, as the final responsibility rests with the reader to implement the emptiness contemplations in a gradual manner so that they can unfold their full potential without creating adverse effects.

The main part of each chapter in this book consists in practice-related explorations of quotations from the Pāli version of the Greater and the Smaller Discourses on Emptiness (the *Mahāsuññatasutta* and the *Cūḷasuññatasutta*). Toward the end of my explorations, I usually present a verse, translated from some other Pāli text, which in one way or another captures in a poetical manner some of the main points to be kept in mind, and a summary of the main points covered in the exploration. After the summary, I return in more detail to the practical implications that have emerged in the course of the chapter. The idea is that, after having read a chapter once, the final section, on "practical instructions," can serve as a reference point for looking up matters relevant to actual meditation. Moreover, the main import of the preceding discussion can be brought to mind by just reading through the summary and/or the verse.

The first part of the verse taken up in the first chapter, entirely dedicated to daily-life dimensions of emptiness practice as the indispensable foundation for going deep in formal sitting, can also serve to convey the main theme underlying this whole book:[5]

> You should contemplate the world as empty,
> Being always mindful.

I. Daily Life

> While abiding by way of this abiding [in emptiness], Ānanda, if the mind of a monastic inclines to walking, then they walk [with this determination]: "Walking like this, no desire and dejection, no bad and unwholesome states will overflow me"; in this way they have clear comprehension of that.[6]

THE ABOVE EXTRACT STEMS from the Greater Discourse on Emptiness (*Mahāsuññatasutta*). The preceding part of the discourse mentions abiding in emptiness internally and externally, wherefore in the above extract I supplemented the indication that the meditative abiding is "[in emptiness]."[7] The distinction into internal and external dimensions of abiding in emptiness reflects the fact that in early Buddhist thought the teaching on emptiness applies internally as well as externally. In other words, the idea of relating the qualification of being empty to persons only and not to other phenomena, found in some later Buddhist traditions, is not relevant for this stage in the history of Buddhist thought. From an early Buddhist perspective all phenomena, without exception, are definitively empty.

The qualification "empty" here points to an absence. In fact, in ancient Indian mathematics the same term can designate "zero."[8] In its early Buddhist usage, to say that something is "empty" is to say that it is "empty of." Even though such absence can take various forms, the key aspect here is that all phenomena are empty of a self, that is, they are empty of a permanent entity of any kind. The resulting insight serves to undermine ego and conceit, as well as possessiveness and selfishness. This sense of emptiness can serve as the main reference point for the daily-life practices explored in the rest of this chapter, which in the final count are about diminishing I-making (= ego) and my-making (= selfishness).

With the instructions in the extract translated above, the Greater Discourse on Emptiness extends abiding in emptiness from formal sitting to other occasions. This can just involve a shift from sitting to walking meditation, but it can equally well become a practice applicable to any posture. In fact, the Greater Discourse on Emptiness presents the same instructions for standing, sitting (which here need not intend only formal meditation but would also comprise sitting down for other purposes), and lying down. The Chinese and Tibetan parallels to the Greater Discourse on Emptiness, however, only describe walking and sitting meditation.[9]

The relevant instructions in the Greater Discourse on Emptiness set out with the indication "while abiding by way of this abiding [in emptiness]." This refers to the previously described abiding in emptiness internally and externally during formal meditation. A very literal reading could lead to the conclusion that one has to do such formal meditation first and then implement the present instructions. When viewed from the perspective of actual practice, however, formal meditation and daily-life application interact and combine. Thus, it is not the case that one comes invariably first and the other always follows. Instead, both support and nourish each other.

Nevertheless, the procedure of presentation in the Greater Discourse on Emptiness is certainly meaningful, as a full appreciation of formal meditation on emptiness provides a convenient foundation for finding modes of applying the same principle to situations outside of sitting meditation. This principle holds similarly for the various perceptions to be developed for formal meditation on emptiness according to the Shorter Discourse on Emptiness. A full appreciation of their potential in being applied to various daily-life situations requires first introducing the perceptions themselves. For this reason, although daily-life application is the theme of the present chapter, I will return to the same topic again and again during subsequent chapters. In fact, relating emptiness to any posture and any activity is of such importance that it merits being taken up time and again, to make sure that its potential receives adequate recognition.

1. Embodied Mindfulness

> While abiding by way of this abiding [in emptiness], Ānanda, if the mind of a monastic inclines to standing, then they stand [with this determination]: "Standing like this, no desire and dejection, no bad and unwholesome states will overflow me"; in this way they have clear comprehension of that.
>
> While abiding by way of this abiding [in emptiness], Ānanda, if the mind of a monastic inclines to sitting, then they sit [with this determination]: "Sitting like this, no desire and dejection, no bad and unwholesome states will overflow me"; in this way they have clear comprehension of that.
>
> While abiding by way of this abiding [in emptiness], Ānanda, if the mind of a monastic inclines to lying down, then they lie down [with this determination]: "Lying down like this, no desire and dejection, no bad and unwholesome states will overflow me"; in this way they have clear comprehension of that.[10]

Together with the extract translated earlier, the instructions in the Greater Discourse on Emptiness comprise the same four postures that are also mentioned in the Discourse on the Establishments of Mindfulness (*Satipaṭṭhānasutta*). In that setting, the meditative task requires being mindful and clearly comprehending which posture we have at present assumed. This calls for a continuous mindful presence with whatever may happen at the bodily level. In fact, the instructions in that discourse add, after the four postures, that the same applies whatever way the body may be positioned.[11]

The relevance of the four establishments of mindfulness to the present instruction can also be seen in the reference to desire and dejection (*abhijjhādomanassa*), which feature regularly in short definitions of the purpose of such mindfulness practice. The same short definitions also mention clearly comprehending (*sampajāna*) as a quality that accompanies mindfulness in this type of practice.[12] In this way, the extract translated above shares with foundational instructions on mindfulness a recognition of the need not only to avoid desire and dejection but also to maintain clear comprehension.

In implementing the above instruction, rooting mindfulness in the presence of the body, in whatever posture, could be combined with clear comprehension directed to our own mental condition. The task of clear comprehension here is to support mindfulness in monitoring the condition of the mind, so as to maintain a condition free from anything unwholesome. This holds for the specific manifestation of any desire or dejection as well as for any other mental state that is bad and unwholesome. In other words, relying on mindfulness and clear comprehension to maintain equanimity in any situation can be considered a key aspect in the cultivation of emptiness.

The reference in the instructions to an *overflowing* of the mind can be understood to intend the potential *influence* exerted by what is apperceived through any of the senses. Due to being established in emptiness, and perhaps more importantly due to remaining established in emptiness, such influence will not be able to impact the mind. In this way, in relation to the relatively ordinary topic of bodily postures, the instruction already points to what in early Buddhist thought is the peak of emptiness: a mind emptied of defilements.

A key for successful arrival at this peak of emptiness is the realization of not self, to be explored in more detail in a subsequent chapter (see below p. 97). In preparation for the practice of not self in formal sitting, the same basic perception of the absence of a self can also be related to all of the four postures. A Pāli discourse describes how appropriation of any of the five aggregates—by way of my-making, I-making, and by postulating a self—will affect each of the four postures: When walking, standing, sitting, and lying down, one who engages in such appropriation is in a predicament similar to a dog bound to a strong post.[13] Due to the bondage to the post, the dog will walk, stand, sit, and lie down close to the post. This description illustrates how the presence of selfing becomes a continuous reference point for any activity and thereby keeps us in continuous bondage, comparable to the poor dog, who would much rather be able to run around freely. Realizing this predicament then invites a different way of going about the four postures, in order to be as free as a dog without a leash. When walking, for example, is it possible to walk without a sense of appropriation? Letting go of a sense of ownership can serve as a very direct application of the teaching on not self. To achieve an experience of freedom from appropriation can take place by simply walking without reifying the sense of "I am" the one who walks, without making this "my" walking. In short, walking without a walker. The same applies equally to the other postures.

Needless to say, there can be a variety of approaches for integrating emptiness into daily life that similarly relate to each of the four postures. Nevertheless, already implementing the present suggestion of attempting to act without a sense of a doer, without the sense of ownership and being in charge, can have a remarkable transformative potential that, even if practiced just on its own, may well offer a substantial contribution to cutting through the bondage of selfing and ego.

2. Talking

> While abiding by way of this abiding [in emptiness], Ānanda, if the mind of a monastic inclines to talking, then [they determine] of whatever talk that is lowly, vulgar, base, ignoble, not beneficial, not leading to disenchantment, dispassion, cessation, peace, direct knowledge, awakening, and Nirvana: "I will not talk such talk, namely talk of kings, talk of robbers, talk of ministers, talk of armies, talk of dangers, talk of battles, talk of food, talk of drink, talk of clothing, talk of beds, talk of garlands, talk of perfumes, talk of relatives, talk of vehicles, talk of villages, talk of towns, talk of cities, talk of countries, talk of women, talk of heroes, talk of streets, talk of wells, talk of the departed, various talk, tales of the world, tales of the sea, and talk about becoming or not becoming such and such"; in this way they have clear comprehension of that.
>
> But, Ānanda, as for that talk that is austere, that is conducive to the mind being free from hindrance, that leads to complete disenchantment, dispassion, cessation, peace, direct knowledge, awakening, and Nirvana, [they determine]: "I will talk

> such talk, namely talk on fewness of wishes, talk on contentment, talk on seclusion, talk on not socializing, talk on making an effort, talk on virtue, talk on concentration, talk on wisdom, talk on liberation, and talk on knowledge and vision of liberation"; in this way they have clear comprehension of that.[14]

The long list of types of talk that should be avoided could be summarized as roughly covering the following main topics:[15] politics, material goods, localities, and various gossip. The point does not seem to be that a conversation related to any of these topics must necessarily be "lowly, vulgar, base, ignoble, not beneficial," etc. Elsewhere among the Pāli discourses and their parallels, a reference to warfare can be part of an instruction on Dharma.[16] The same holds for a flower garland, which features in a simile describing a pretty youth delighted at receiving such a garland.[17] Such references do not turn the respective teaching into something censurable.

Instead of adopting a literal reading of the listing as prohibiting certain topics in principle, its function can rather be understood to exemplify what usually comes up when we engage in communication that is lowly, vulgar, base, ignoble, and not beneficial. It is the latter that is central; in fact, it is possible to broach other topics, even some of those mentioned above as commendable, in ways that are lowly and not beneficial. For example, we may pride ourselves in front of others on having few wishes, being contented, or living in seclusion and then disparage those perceived as not having these qualities to the same degree. This would fall into the category of ignoble ways of conversation that are not beneficial.

It follows that emptiness in matters of conversation would be less about the topics chosen—although these of course also matter—and more about the intention motivating our engaging in communication. In other words, is our engaging in a conversation done for the purpose of leading to "disenchantment, dispassion, cessation, peace, direct knowledge, awakening, and Nirvana"? Understood in this way, abiding in emptiness involves a reorientation of our conversational activities, whereby it becomes another mindfulness practice. Once the task is not just implementation of a prohibition of certain topics, the actual undertaking of the practice described above calls for a continuous, mindful monitoring of any conversation, in order to notice when it is about to stray off into what is lowly, etc. In addition, the overall attitude toward communication changes. The primary interest is no longer in accumulating all kinds of informational details or celebrating our own subjectivity, both of which can take up so much time and energy in the contemporary setting with its internet, social networks, etc. The crucial question and orientation point is much rather how far a particular conversation will support emptying the mind of defilements.

3. Thoughts

> While abiding by way of this abiding [in emptiness], Ānanda, if the mind of a monastic inclines to thinking, then [they determine] of whatever thoughts that are lowly, vulgar, base, ignoble, not beneficial, not leading to disenchantment, dispassion, cessation, peace, direct knowledge, awakening, and Nirvana: "I will not think such thoughts, namely thought of sensuality, thought of ill will, and thought of harming"; in this way they have clear comprehension of that.
>
> But, Ānanda, as for thoughts that are noble, leading onward, leading one who implements them to the complete ending of *dukkha*, [they determine]: "I will think such thoughts, namely thought of renunciation, thought of non-ill will, and thought of non-harming"; in this way they have clear comprehension of that.[18]

The Greater Discourse on Emptiness continues after the above extract with various other topics. Since none of these begins with a reference to "abiding by way of this abiding [in emptiness]," these appear to be not as directly relevant to the topic of emptiness meditation as the parts translated above. The instructions that do begin with this reference thus comprise abiding in emptiness in all postures, while talking, and in relation to thinking activity. The very fact that thoughts are explicitly taken up for such purposes shows that emptiness practice does not invariably require a mind empty of thoughts. Although mental tranquility offers a substantial contribution to the practices to be explored in the next chapters, the basic principle holds there as well: thoughts are not a problem per se. Instead, the crucial question is what type of thoughts are in the mind.

The basic distinction drawn in the extract translated above concerns the presence and absence of sensuality, ill will, and harming. These correspond to the key aspects underlying right intention, the second factor in the noble eightfold path, which sets the appropriate context for meditation on emptiness in early Buddhist thought. This calls for further exploration.

The guiding principle of the noble eightfold path is the first path factor of right view, which for purposes of meditation practice can conveniently take the form of the four noble truths.[19] Apparently inspired by an ancient Indian scheme of medical diagnosis,[20] the four noble truths call for a recognition of the presence of *dukkha* (Sanskrit: *duḥkha*), together with acknowledging that our own craving makes a rather substantial contribution to this state of affairs. The third and fourth truth then concern the vision of freedom from *dukkha/duḥkha* and the path of practice leading to that goal, which is none other than the eightfold path. In this way, right view is the guiding factor of this path and at the same time provides its overall contextualization. This presentation points to a continuous feedback loop, where what initially may have been a mere theoretical appreciation of the four noble truths becomes something ever more embodied, lived, and realized, thereby strengthening the basic directive provided by right view and deepening inner clarity in understanding the overall contextual setting of progress on the path.

The presence of right view provides the directive for right intention as the second path factor, in terms of the absence of sensuality, ill will, and harming, also mentioned in the extract from the Greater Discourse on Emptiness translated above. Before turning to this in more detail, the remaining path factors can be surveyed briefly. The next three factors of the eightfold path extend the perspective afforded by right view to various activities, comprising speech, action, and livelihood. This conveys that the proper attitude, which in the present context can in particular take the form of a growing insight into emptiness, needs to pervade all aspects of our life.

The remaining path factors are more specifically concerned with mental training. Right effort calls for overcoming detrimental mental states and nourishing their wholesome counterparts. Ways to implement that in relation to emptiness will come up in subsequent chapters of my exploration. Right mindfulness concerns the mental quality that is perhaps the most important one for successfully cultivating the emptiness meditations described in this book. Right concentration completes the section of the eightfold path relevant to mental training by way of mental composure and tranquility. Although this last factor has often been taken to imply the necessity to master absorption attainment, a close comparative study of the early discourses suggests this view needs revision. What concentration requires above all to become of the *right* type, whatever its depth, is the directive of right view and the collaboration of the other path factors.[21] Without thereby in any way intending to deny the value of deeply concentrated states of absorption, these are not indispensable for implementing the eightfold path or for cultivating the emptiness meditations described in this book.

The three modalities of right intention that emerge within the context of the eightfold path—the absence of thoughts of sensuality, ill will, and harming—broach topics of considerable importance for abiding in emptiness. The first of the three involves renunciation instead of sensuality, the former being noble and leading to liberation, as the Greater Discourse on Emptiness clarifies, whereas the latter is ignoble and leads away from awakening. Although this does not mean that celibacy is a must, it does require a reorientation of our priorities away from a consumerist attitude and the quest for sensual gratification. Several of the stages in the gradual meditation on emptiness, to be taken up in subsequent chapters, offer substantial help for such a reorientation. Opportunities to cultivate renunciation can be identified in any daily-life situation, be it in relation to food, desire for comfort, wish for company, etc. It is right at the time when our expectations in these respects are not being fulfilled that emptiness practice can unfold its liberating potential.

The other two modalities of right intention concern the absence of ill will and harming. Expressed positively, these correspond to the attitudes of *mettā* (Sanskrit: *maitrī*), which could be rendered as "benevolence" or "loving kindness," and compassion (Pāli and Sanskrit: *karuṇā*). The proposed correlation between *mettā/maitrī* and the absence of ill will as well as between compassion and the absence of harming follows a general mode of presentation in the early discourses that equates the four divine abodes (Pāli and Sanskrit: *brahmavihāra*) to the absence of those mental conditions that are directly opposed to them. One who has fully cultivated *mettā/maitrī*, for example, will no longer be completely overwhelmed by ill will.[22] The same holds for compassion in relation to harming. Regarding the last case, it may be opportune to note that the early Buddhist notion of compassion does not involve taking on the pain of others.[23] Instead, it entails the fervent wish for the absence of harm, that is, for freedom from whatever is afflictive. By being oriented toward such freedom, rather than remaining focused on the painful nature of the affliction, such compassion can even combine with joy, namely the joy of doing what we can to alleviate and prevent harm.

The task of not thinking thoughts of ill will and harming, described in the extract translated above, is not merely about implementing an abstinence. In fact, thoughts often arise without previous deliberation. It follows that freedom from thoughts of ill will and harming cannot be achieved through just trying to enforce control. For this reason, there is a need to train the mind in renunciation and in the divine abodes, so that there is less scope in the first place for the opposite type of detrimental thoughts to arise. The basic principle here is that thoughts are closely interrelated with inclinations of the mind.[24] Dwelling in a particular mental condition will encourage the arising of corresponding thoughts and forestall the frequent manifestation of their opposites. In terms of right effort, there is a need to complement confronting what is unwholesome with cultivating what is wholesome.

In this way, the above instruction can conveniently be taken as an occasion for encouraging the cultivation of these two divine abodes. Such a cultivation is particularly appropriate as a complement to the gradual meditative entry into emptiness, especially if meditation on these two divine abodes takes inspiration from the standard way described in the early discourses. Such descriptions differ from a widespread approach to *brahmavihāra* meditation, which requires bringing to mind specific individuals toward whom the respective divine abode will then be directed.[25] Without in any way intending to deny the practical benefits of such a person-oriented approach, an alternative way of practice inspired by the standard description in the early discourses could take the form of arousing the divine abode without necessarily relying on a particular circumscribed object. This can then lead over to a boundless radiation of the divine abode in all directions. Such a form of meditative radiation, whose practical implementation I have described in detail elsewhere,[26] would be an expedient way of doing justice to the alternative appellation of the *brahmavihāras* as states that are "boundless" or "immeasurable" (*appamāṇa/apramāṇa*). The same would also tie in well with several of the perceptions to be cultivated in the course of the gradual meditation on emptiness, as these also involve modalities of meditative abiding that do not rely on focusing on a circumscribed object.

The resemblance between the divine abodes and the gradual entry into emptiness in matters of meditative cultivation is such that an alternative approach, not explored in this book, can take the form of proceeding through all four divine abodes and then shifting from the last divine abode of equanimity directly to the perception of infinite space, which is the third of the perceptions in the gradual meditation on emptiness. This approach sidesteps the two previous perceptions in this gradual meditation, which are related to the forest and to earth.

An advantage of this approach is the ease of the meditative transition from abiding in boundless equanimity, the fourth *brahmavihāra*, to abiding in infinite space. All this requires is a subtle shift in perspective. Another and perhaps even more important advantage is that a cultivation of the divine abodes provides a firm grounding of emptiness practice, which helps avoid possible pitfalls and problems that can occur with meditation on emptiness, something I briefly mentioned in the introduction (see above p. 3). Since the divine abodes have a rather crucial contribution to make to emptiness meditation in this way, I would like to recommend in quite definite terms that they should be considered indispensable. This holds at least for the first two, which come up implicitly in the extract translated above.

A previous cultivation of the divine abodes supports the actual practice of emptiness meditation by way of establishing a basic degree of inner integration and a healthy way of relating to others. This is vital for successfully navigating the deconstruction strategies explored in the subsequent chapters. Whenever these become too challenging, there needs to be another practice to return to for grounding ourselves. This is precisely what the boundless abiding in the divine abodes can provide.

The divine abodes exemplify in a very down-to-earth manner what, in the final count, emptiness is about. With the meditative approach described in the next chapters, there is a danger of mishandling emptiness experiences. This can manifest in becoming aloof and indifferent, even arrogant and reckless. This danger can be countered through regular practice of the divine abodes. In fact, genuine practice and realization of emptiness manifests in an opening of the heart rather than leading to its closure. *Mettā/maitrī* and compassion are in a way the other side of the coin of emptiness; the two sides need each other to flourish. *Mettā/maitrī* and compassion without emptiness can become exhausting, particularly when witnessing various instances of suffering becomes overwhelming. But emptiness without *mettā/maitrī* and compassion is even worse, as it can become toxic or barren. For this reason, I strongly recommend making the divine abodes an integral part of our regular emptiness meditation. Their natural manifestation in daily life can serve as a measuring rod of progress in the realization of emptiness. This is what it all boils down to: emptiness in the form of freedom from defilements. Such freedom has its positive counterpart in active expressions of the divine abodes by body, speech, and mind.

By way of concluding the present survey of daily-life dimensions of emptiness, I would like to come back to a topic mentioned at the outset, namely the all-pervasive nature of emptiness in early Buddhist thought as a reference to the whole world, internal as well as external. This combines with a reference to mindfulness in a verse that can be taken as an orientation point for the practices described in this chapter. According to this verse, mindfully contemplating the world as empty leads beyond the vision of the King of Death, that is, beyond being afflicted by what for the majority of human beings is the most threatening thing in their whole life: their own mortality.[27]

You should contemplate the world as empty,
Being always mindful ...
The King of Death does not see
One who contemplates the world like this.

4. Summary

The Greater Discourse on Emptiness provides instructions on how abiding in emptiness can be related to daily life. The relevant indications, which can be relied on to complement the instructions on formal meditation given in the Smaller Discourse on Emptiness, begin with the four postures of the body. This instruction invites combining an embodied form of mindfulness with clear comprehension directed toward keeping the mind empty of defilements. In addition to that, investigation can target the central peg on which defilements hang: selfing. Letting go of self-referentiality while being in any bodily posture can become a powerful implementation of emptiness and carry considerable transformative potential. This can take the form of simply walking without a walker (etc.), that is, without construing the sense of an "I" who walks and without appropriating the walking in any way.

Even conversations can be related to emptiness, by way of ensuring that these are ennobling and liberative, rather than ignoble and fettering. Emptiness in relation to thoughts exhibits a close relationship to the second factor of the noble eightfold path: right intention. Forestalling the arising of thoughts that are opposed to this path factor can take the form of engendering an attitude of renunciation and cultivating the divine abodes of *mettā/maitrī* and compassion. Such cultivation can take the form of a boundless radiation in all directions, which provides a convenient foundation for, and complement to, the similarly boundless perceptions of the gradual meditation on emptiness.

The divine abodes offer a rather substantial contribution to emptiness practice. They provide a foundation to which we can return whenever emptiness perceptions threaten to become destabilizing. Moreover, they forestall the potential danger of misapprehending emptiness and misusing the perceptions described in the remainder of this book as ways of cultivating aloofness and indifference. True emptiness manifests in an open heart rather than in a closed one. It calls for emptying the mind of defilements, which has its natural expression in a flourishing of the divine abodes.

5. Practical Instructions

Here and elsewhere, under the heading of practical instructions I try to draw out in more detail the practice dimension of the material surveyed in each chapter. This can at times involve some degree of repetition, as several topics have already been covered in the preceding exploration of the relevant discourse quotations.

A key element in putting into practice the above indications is embodied mindfulness. The basic point here is that for most meditators to be able to navigate the challenges of situations outside of formal meditation, there needs to be some support to ensure continuity of mindfulness. Contrary to recommendations often given in contemporary times, the early discourses do not recommend the breath for such purposes. The standard instructions for mindfulness of breathing stipulate seclusion and the sitting posture, making it clear that the practice described is meant for formal meditation.[28] This holds in particular for the sixteen steps of mindfulness of breathing described in the discourses.

But even just being aware of the breath as such can be challenging as a daily-life practice, simply because the process of breathing is a subtle phenomenon and, at least when breathing is normal, not easily noticed. It requires some effort and often also some degree of focus. Yet, maintaining such a focus can easily interfere with other duties in an average life situation. Therefore, using just a focus on the breath as a foundation for continuity of mindfulness in daily life is not a particularly easy option. If we wish to maintain a relationship to the breath outside of formal sitting, a better option would be to embed mindfulness of the breath in whole-body awareness, rather than cultivating an exclusive focus on the breath. In this way, attending to the breath would become merely a part of being aware of the whole body, avoiding an exclusive focus and thereby becoming less challenging in daily life.

In fact, the whole body is a considerably more promising support for continuity of mindfulness in any situation. The body in its entirety is more easily noticed, compared to the breath alone. Moreover, due to being itself a broad object, it encourages a broader type of attention instead of a narrow focus. In addition, much of what needs to be done in daily life involves the body in one form or another. Combining that activity with a general awareness of the whole body does not introduce a particularly challenging task. Furthermore, if mindfulness of the whole body is present throughout whatever needs to be done, that activity will usually be performed in a better way and with better results. In other words, rather than creating stress due to requiring attentional mental resources, this type of approach easily harmonizes with what needs to be done and pays off in better performance.

This much holds even for the case of being in some conversation, to stay with the example broached above. Awareness of our bodily posture, perhaps seated at a round table discussion or a conference, can introduce an element of centeredness and calmness that will support and strengthen whatever we have to say. Listening to another with some attention resting on the body will make it easier to stay calm when someone else is rambling on about what does not really seem relevant, enabling us to allow the space for the other to have their say rather than intervening too early out of a sense of boredom and annoyance. Time spent listening to another is never lost, as long as this is done with whole-body awareness.

An additional benefit is also that whole-body awareness tends to harmonize the signals sent by our own bodily behavior with what happens on the conscious level of our mind. This is simply because we will notice quickly if some irritation, for example, expresses itself at the bodily level through posture, movements of our limbs, or even facial expression. Often enough others pick up and react to such signals. If these have not been noted by us, this can derail a whole conversation. Practicing whole-body awareness helps to stay attuned to this level of communication, which usually is noticed more easily with others than in our own case.

All of the above examples offer practical implementations of meditation on emptiness based on whole-body awareness. Such implementation is of course not confined to the body. In fact, the instructions make it clear that a central task is clear comprehension of what is happening in the mind. Becoming aware of the mind is indeed central, so the point is only that whole-body awareness provides a particularly convenient grounding and foundation for turning to the mind and remaining aware of it.

Besides benefiting from a grounding in whole-body awareness, this requires cultivating the ability to see through the current stream of thoughts and associations in order to recognize—to comprehend clearly—the underlying mental current. The instructions for cultivating mindfulness in relation to any posture mention "desire and dejection" and states that are "bad and unwholesome," two qualifications that appear to function as near synonyms. As a simplification for actual practice, we could be on the lookout for likes and dislikes (= "desire and dejection") and try to note the manifestation of defilements in general (= "bad and unwholesome states"), which usually have some form of liking or disliking as their starting point. Detecting the onset of such reactions by way of liking or disliking relies on our familiarity with those symptoms that manifest when we are about to get caught up in reactivity and are on the verge of an unwholesome reaction. Needless to say, the sooner this is recognized the easier it is remedied, simply because the defilement in question is only at an incipient stage and has not yet had time to gather strength. In this way, mindfulness related to bodily postures can result in a powerful approach for making emptiness something directly beneficial in any situation.

Such general applicability extends even to the realm of conversations, which in contemporary times would include internet, social networks, emails, etc. Throughout, there is a need to adopt the proper orientation in order for such activities to become supportive of emptiness abiding, rather than running counter to it. This calls for a continuity in embodied mindfulness and the effort to pause for a moment before talking or writing a message. Just a brief pause for recollecting our overall aspiration and checking if what is about to be said or written is in alignment with that.

The application of emptiness to thought opens up a perspective of practice that is about as important for the emptiness meditations described in the remainder of this book as embodied mindfulness. This is the cultivation of the divine abodes, in particular *mettā/maitrī* and compassion. In the present context, these build on a foundation in renunciation, by way of reorienting our whole lifestyle toward a higher purpose and aspiration, in contrast to a hedonistic attitude whose concerns are just to ensure maximizing sensual gratification. In order to provide meditative support for thoughts of non-ill will and non-harming, and perhaps more importantly for the emptiness meditations taken up in the remainder of this book, formal cultivation of *mettā/maitrī* and compassion recommend themselves.

Actual practice can begin by arousing the respective mental attitude: *mettā/maitrī* toward all, being the very opposite of anger and ill will, and compassion toward all, being the very opposite of harming and cruelty. If needs be, this can rely on a particular phrase or phrases, but sooner rather than later it would be good to shift from phrase(s) to the actual attitude as such. Such a shift involves a transition from doing to being, in the sense of proceeding from an arousal of the divine abode, with the help of whatever crutch we may find useful for this purpose, to just abiding in it and allowing our whole being to be pervaded by the respective mental attitude. This type of shift from actively generating a particular mental attitude to fully embodying it is of continuous relevance to the emptiness practices described in subsequent chapters. Throughout, a progression leads from a more active arousal to effortlessly abiding and fully embodying the same attitude or insight.

Based on such abiding in a divine abode, we then open up in all directions, as a way of establishing boundlessness. Such opening up is not a forceful matter, but more comparable to a light that has been surrounded by curtains on all sides, and now these curtains are softly and gently withdrawn. The inner light of the divine abode shines however far it wishes to shine; there is no need to push or use force. The task is not to shine the divine abode as far as possible but much rather to ensure that no limitations are imposed. There should be no exceptions, in the sense of cultivating the divine abode to everyone except such and such person(s). As long as no exemptions are made, the condition of boundlessness has been accomplished, which in terms of my above simile is to withdraw the curtains so that the light can shine unhindered.

Abiding in this condition of the mind can rely on the continuity of embodied awareness as well as on noting the process of breathing, as long as the latter is done without focusing on the breath to the exclusion of everything else. Experiencing the alternations between inhalations and exhalations as an integral part of whole-body awareness can help to strengthen continuity. With every inhalation, there can be a bit more emphasis on the actual quality of the divine abode. With every exhalation, there can be a bit more emphasis on the boundless condition of the mind, on the absence of any limitation. This suggestion does not commend an either/or approach. Instead, it is just about a slight difference in emphasis. It also does not entail any influencing of the breath itself; breathing stays natural. The idea is only to give mindfulness slightly different observational angles in order to create some variation in the experience that can forestall the arising of boredom leading to distraction. Once the meditation comes to its natural conclusion, it would be good to share the merits of our practice in whatever way we are accustomed to do so.

II. Seclusion

Ānanda, earlier as well as now I often abide by way of abiding in emptiness. Ānanda, it is just like this palace of Migāra's mother, which is empty of elephants, cows, horses, and mares, empty of gold and silver, empty of a gathering of women and men, and yet there is this non-emptiness, namely the [perceptual] oneness in dependence on the monastic community. Ānanda, in the same way, not attending to the perception of the village and not attending to the perception of people, a monastic attends to oneness in dependence on the perception of the forest. Their mind enters upon, is pleased with, settles on, and is devoted to the perception of the forest.

They understand like this: "Whatever disturbances there could be in dependence on the perception of the village, these are not present here. Whatever disturbances there could be in dependence on the perception of people, these are not present here. There is just this remainder of disturbance, namely the oneness in dependence on the perception of the forest."

They understand: "This perceptual range is empty of the perception of the village"; and they understand: "This perceptual range is empty of the perception of people. There is just this non-emptiness, namely the oneness in dependence on the perception of the forest."

Thus, they contemplate it as empty of what is indeed not there, and they understand that what remains there is still present: "It is there." Ānanda, like this there also comes to be for them this genuine, undistorted, and purified entry into emptiness.[29]

1. The Buddha's Abiding

With this chapter, my exploration shifts from the Greater to the Smaller Discourse on Emptiness, whose instructions are particularly relevant to formal meditation. Whereas in the previous chapter I introduced emptiness practice during daily life based on sections of the Greater Discourse on Emptiness that explicitly relate a meditative abiding in emptiness to activities outside of formal meditation, for exploring formal sitting meditation as such in this and subsequent chapters I rely on the Shorter Discourse on Emptiness. The introductory narration of this discourse reports that the Buddha's attendant Ānanda had approached his teacher in order to verify the correctness of his recollection that on a former occasion the Buddha had stated that he often abides in emptiness. After confirming that Ānanda remembered correctly, the passage translated above falls into place. The implication would be that engaging in the whole practice described in the remainder of the discourse is a way of emulating the Buddha's own abiding in emptiness.

This starting point in an emulation of the Buddha can be taken as a reference point for our own individual motivation. Although the paths aimed at arahantship and at Buddhahood differ in several respects, the profoundly inspiring example set by the Buddha is their common orientation point. The possibility to follow in his footsteps should be of similar inspiration to any practicing Buddhist. Of course, a difference not to be ignored is to what extent we wish to attain Nirvana in this very life. In order to grant due recognition to differences in this respect, in the concluding step of this gradual meditative entry into emptiness I will endeavor to make it sufficiently clear at which point those who do not feel inspired to take the plunge into Nirvana should not take their practice further.

Apart from this final step, however, the meditative trajectory of the gradual meditation on emptiness has much to offer for Buddhist practitioners with various motivations and coming from a range of different traditions. This trajectory proceeds from perception of the forest to the perceptions of earth, infinite space, infinite consciousness, nothingness, and signlessness. Each of these perceptions has considerable potential for deepening our understanding of emptiness and our ability to embody it.

The teachings of early Buddhism are the historical beginning of all Buddhist traditions and thus can serve as a shared reference point. In the present case, as already mentioned in the introduction, the discourse under discussion is fortunately extant not only in Pāli but also in Chinese and Tibetan parallel versions. The relevant teachings thereby form part of what, from a traditional perspective, are considered the canonical scriptures of the South and Southeast Asian, East Asian, and Himalayan Buddhist traditions.

The instructions for the first step in learning how to emulate the Buddha's abiding in emptiness take up the present situation, just as it is. In the case of the conversation between the Buddha and Ānanda, this was a monastic dwelling donated by Visākhā (Sanskrit: Viśākhā), also known by the title "Migāra's mother."[30] The monastic dwelling was situated in a park outside the eastern gate of Sāvatthī (Sanskrit: Śrāvastī). From the viewpoint of the Buddha and Ānanda being in that place, and perhaps having earlier that day been to the city of Sāvatthī to beg for their food, it is natural to draw a contrast between the busy life in town and their secluded dwelling in the forest of this park. The seclusion they experienced in this way involves the absence of "elephants, cows, horses, and mares," reflecting the type of traffic one would encounter in an ancient Indian city. Similarly absent are "gold and silver," items whose possession is prohibited to monastics, thus representing lay commerce. Also absent is any "gathering of women and men," as the only human beings present at that time and in that place were members of the community of monastics. Their similarity in appearance, due to being shaven headed and wearing simple robes, results in a perceptual experience of oneness that favorably contrasts to the items just mentioned.

The overall thrust of this first part of the instruction takes the form of applying the basic sense of emptiness as an absence right to the actual location. Even though the ensuing meditative trajectory leads to profound states of meditation, each of its steps has a direct bearing on the here and now. This undercurrent is present from the outset, evident in the sense of immediacy with which, according to the above passage, the Buddha turns from his own lofty abiding in emptiness to the actual setting as a demonstration of how emptiness can be directly related to the here and now.

The demonstration given in this way can be read as an encouragement to use whatever circumstances may present themselves in a pragmatical manner. The main point would be simply to attend to absence. Wherever we find ourselves right now: What is absent? Such inquiry can conveniently be related to our present experience without having to stick to the list given in the discourse. The instructions simply reflect the setting of the discourse and need not be taken to restrict the range of objects whose absence we may notice. In other words, anything that is noticeably not there could in principle be attended to as absent and thereby as exemplifying the welcome presence of seclusion appropriate for formal meditation.

2. The Perception of the Forest

A difference between the parallel versions of the Smaller Discourse on Emptiness emerges in regard to this first step. Whereas the Pāli version combines perception of the monastic community with perception of the forest in a single treatment, the two parallels extant in Chinese and Tibetan present these in a way that gives the impression of two distinct steps.[31] In a way, both presentations make sense. Nevertheless, it seems possible, although not certain, that the presentation in the Chinese and Tibetan versions results from a textual expansion in their common ancestor in oral transmission, whereby the repetitive treatment of the ensuing steps was also applied to the perception of the monastic community. Be that as it may, an advantage of the presentation in the Pāli version is that the resultant progression leads more directly to the notion of seclusion, which is indeed the central connotation of the perception of the forest.[32] From a practical perspective, a direct approach to practicing the above translated instructions would thus be to attend to whatever absence of distractions our own situation affords.

A reference to the perception of the forest as a means for achieving oneness of the mind can be found in another two otherwise-unrelated

Pāli discourses.[33] The relevant passages report the Buddha describing a monastic who is sitting in the forest but is nodding off. Yet, the Buddha anticipates that this monastic will dispel the drowsiness and, by attending to the perception of the forest, achieve oneness (of the mind). This contrasts favorably to another monastic, mentioned in the preceding part of the two discourses, who is sitting in concentration but in the vicinity of a village. The Buddha anticipates that this monastic will soon be disturbed by someone else and thereby incur a loss of concentration. After describing the case of the drowsy monastic, the two discourses continue with the case of another monastic sitting in concentration in the forest, in which case the Buddha anticipates that this monastic will progress and liberate the mind, as well as protect the liberated mind. The point that emerges in this way is that, due to not being in forest seclusion, someone who is concentrated risks losing it. In contrast, due to being in forest seclusion, someone not concentrated will gain it, and someone concentrated will progress further. This description thereby provides a very clear endorsement of forest seclusion in support of formal meditation practice.

Perhaps this passage could also be taken as an inspiration to set up one's life in such a way as to facilitate the manifestation of conditions suitable for pursuing formal meditation and periodical retreat. In other words, doing justice to the call for seclusion could take the form of avoiding pursuits or undertakings that stand good chances at preventing us from engaging in formal practice and undertaking retreats. Such a call could take as its orientation point some of the topics mentioned above in the instructions on cultivating emptiness in relation to talking (see above p. 10), which also mention, in addition to seclusion itself, fewness of wishes, contentment, and not socializing.

The importance of living in seclusion appears to have been evident to the Buddha himself already during the time of his quest for awakening. A Pāli discourse and its parallel depict how at that time he dedicated himself wholeheartedly to living in forest seclusion and how he faced the challenges of such a lifestyle as part of his gradual progress toward eventually gaining of concentration and liberating insight.[34]

In view of these indications, it is hardly a surprise to find that the forest features in the standard description of how someone withdraws into seclusion to engage in formal sitting meditation.[35] In addition to the forest, such descriptions mention the root of a tree and an empty house. The last reference employs the notion of emptiness in its most basic sense, namely as a simple reference to an absence. The empty house is devoid of other people or sources of distraction and for this reason affords the type of seclusion that can alternatively be gained by going into a forest.

Seclusion as such can be of an external or an internal type. This concords with a general characteristic of early Buddhist thought to see the internal world of the mind and the external world outside as closely interrelated, to the extent that a journey through different meditative attainments mirrors a journey through the corresponding cosmological realms and vice versa.[36] The standard descriptions of the gradual path regularly combine a description of external seclusion—a forest, the root of a tree, or an empty house—with a pointer at inner seclusion, namely the absence of the five hindrances.[37] Although these are not mentioned explicitly in the instructions translated at the outset of this chapter, it does seem meaningful to extend the perception of the forest to include the main task that anyone who withdraws to meditate needs to master: overcoming the five hindrances in order to gain the type of mental seclusion that is indispensable for meditation to flourish.

3. Mental Seclusion

Overcoming the five hindrances of sensual desire, anger or ill will, sloth-and-torpor, restlessness-and-worry, and doubt can thus be taken as representing the mental dimension of seclusion, in the sense of being an important precondition for successful meditation. These five hindrances have been singled out from the various detrimental states recognized in the early Buddhist analysis of the mind for their particular propensity to *hinder* its proper functioning.[38] The mental conditions selected in this way cover seven states altogether, since in the case of the third and fourth hindrances two problematic qualities have been listed together, presumably due to their similar effects on the mind: sloth, as a state of laziness and boredom, combines with torpor, as physical tiredness and fatigue;

restlessness, as a general condition of agitation, combines with worry, as mental apprehension often caused by a specific problem.

In the present context, after surveying our condition of physical seclusion, it would be good to check in on the present condition of the mind in order to ascertain whether it is under the power of one of these five hindrances. Should this be the case, the time has come to employ appropriate antidotes that our past experience has shown to be particularly effective. Once the five hindrances are at least temporarily absent—the question here is not to fuss about very minor traces in the mind but rather to consider absence to stand for not being overpowered by a hindrance—the resultant type of mental seclusion can be given full attention.

Another mental quality that would also fit the notion of mental seclusion is contentment. This could even be viewed as an implementation of the perception of the monastic community, mentioned in the instructions, given that the idea of going forth is, at least in principle, to embark on a full-time training in contentment and in living a frugal life. Moreover, cultivating contentment can be related to the principle of renunciation, mentioned in the previous chapter as one of the three modalities of commendable thought for one who abides in emptiness (see above p. 10).

The main attitude of contentment enables remaining equally at ease with what is present and what is absent. As a general attitude that is of course also applicable outside of the monastic context, contentment does not imply an encouragement to turn a blind eye to problems but rather calls for doing what is reasonably possible and then letting go and letting be.[39] In relation to the main theme of the instructions, physical seclusion, it is indeed meaningful to try to establish as much seclusion from potential disturbances as possible before sitting down to meditate. At that point, however, an attitude of contentment should take over in order to be able to face any disturbance that may still manifest with ease and balance. Although it is helpful to establish proper external conditions, it is perhaps even more important to establish proper inner conditions. It will not do to make meditation practice depend on externals. To some extent these can be taken care of in advance, but then there needs to be a shift in perspective by seeing problems as learning opportunities, in particular as opportunities to develop patience and contentment, as well as in a way inviting insight into the ultimately unsatisfactory nature of all experiences.

A useful attitude to problems that cannot be avoided is to remind ourselves that it could be worse. An implementation of this strategy for cultivating contentment and patience can find inspiration in the description of a monastic who was planning to live in a region known for its fierce inhabitants. On being asked by the Buddha what he would do if people were to abuse him, the monastic is on record for responding that he would appreciate that he is not being given a fist blow.[40] The Buddha reportedly continued pressing the same issue by asking what the monastic would do if he should receive a fist blow. In that case, the monastic was ready to appreciate that he was not experiencing a clod being thrown at him. The discourse continues with ever worse scenarios, yet the monastic continues to come up with reflections along the lines that it could be worse. The Buddha was satisfied with these answers, as with the kind of attitude evinced in this way the monastic in question was able to face any challenge patiently.

The applicability of this strategy is not confined to external challenges. A fruitful arena for exploring the potential of paying attention to the absence of what would be worse is the experience of disease and pain. Suppose one part of the body is in pain. This almost inevitably leads to a complete focus on the afflicted part, as if the whole person had been reduced to the area of the body that hurts. In such a situation, paying attention to those parts of the body that are not aching presently can be a remarkably helpful tool, broadening our perspective and alleviating the mental suffering caused by the pain. Should the ache be all over the body, the same basic strategy can be employed, the difference being that, instead of being applied to parts of the body, it is rather applied to other potential afflictions and diseases, which are absent. With a little bit of creativity, it will be possible to achieve a similar broadening of perspective and diminishing of mental suffering, based on the same procedure of attending to absence.

The treatment suggested for the case of pain could also be employed for noise experienced while meditating. If a particular noise becomes disturbing, a helpful strategy can be to bring to mind the many other noises that are actually absent. Or else, if something that happened recently keeps occupying the mind, a short reminder that the person(s) or the particular matter is absent right now can go a long way in helping the mind to settle. In this and other ways, paying attention to absence can become a fruitful meditative strategy with clear-cut results in learning to face problems with ease and balance.

4. Empty of Disturbances

The basic implication of emptiness to convey that something is absent features regularly in the instructions for all the steps in the gradual approach to emptiness. The pattern throughout is to recognize what has been transcended as absent. This recognition has two dimensions: the absence of a potential source of disturbance and the understanding that such absence is a form of emptiness. In addition to acknowledging these two dimensions of absence, the instructions also invite an acknowledgment of what is still present. Due to being still present, it is a potential source of disturbance, and it is also a form of non-emptiness, so to say. In the case of the perception of the forest, for example, what is absent are perceptions of the village and of people. Hence, the perception of the forest is empty of these. Still present, however, is the very perception of the forest. Hence, the present step in the gradual meditation on emptiness is not empty of that perception of the forest.

This concern with absence and presence shows a very practical side to emptiness. Rather than being some kind of abstract notion, it is much rather about a quality, namely about being "empty of." The instructions in fact use the adjective "empty" more often than the noun "emptiness," and for a proper understanding of their implications it can be quite helpful to keep the emphasis on an adjective or a quality. In other words, the instructions do not involve some metaphysical or ontological entity, but simply the quality of absence. This elegantly sidesteps the problem of whether emptiness is something apart from or else identical with what it designates. Just as being wet is not apart from water and being hot not apart from fire, so being empty is not apart from phenomena. As already noted in relation to the Greater Discourse on Emptiness, in early Buddhist thought there is no restriction regarding the applicability of the quality of being empty, such as being only applicable to persons. As the remainder of the meditative trajectory will make unmistakably clear, the quality of being empty applies to all phenomena without exception.

The qualification of being empty has a somewhat different placement in the parallels.[41] Whereas the Pāli version first takes up the topic of potential disturbances and then turns to the theme of emptiness, the Chinese and Tibetan parallels adopt the opposite sequence. From a practical perspective, the sequence found in the Chinese and Tibetan versions is appealing, as it first takes up the central topic of emptiness and then rounds off such contemplation by bringing in what appears to be an implementation of one of the three characteristics of all that is conditioned: *dukkha/duḥkha*.

The Pāli term rendered above as "disturbance" is *daratha*. The Tibetan version speaks of *nyon mongs pa'i gnas*, which according to Skilling (1997, 352) appears to be a rendering of Sanskrit *daratha*, for which he proposes the rendering "discomfort." The Chinese version employs *píláo*,[42] which conveys a sense of "weariness," "tiredness," or "fatigue."

From a practical perspective, although village life may indeed be qualified a disturbance or discomfort in contrast to forest seclusion, or else be considered a source of weariness, a literal understanding of the same qualification does not seem to fit equally well the perceptions to be explored in the next chapters. The problem is that disturbance, weariness, etc., convey a sense of coarseness that does not align easily with the rather subtle experiences in the later trajectory of the entry into emptiness.

The term *daratha* can also convey the nuance of being heated up. In some Pāli texts this sense of the term stands in direct contrast to Nirvana,[43] which is regularly associated with coolness in the early discourses. Although I have not been able to come up with a rendering of *daratha* that does justice to this nuance,[44] perhaps it would be possible to keep it in mind for actual practice. The main point that emerges from the proposed understanding is that all the meditative perceptions described in the discourse fall short of the final goal of Nirvana; they still partake of the *hotness* of being conditioned and fall short of the *coolness* of the unconditioned. In other words, the reference to a disturbance still present can be read to convey a sense of "not yet," serving as an injunction to proceed further to what is even more peaceful and liberating.

From the viewpoint of the three characteristics of impermanence, lack of satisfactoriness (*dukkha/duḥkha*), and lack of a self, the last of the three is clearly the one given central importance in the Smaller Discourse on Emptiness. Impermanence becomes prominent in the final part, as a way of completing the maturation of insight in such a way as to lead to the breakthrough to the unconditioned. The quality of failing to provide lasting satisfaction, *dukkha/duḥkha*, in turn is woven into the background of each step in the meditative trajectory through this recurrent reminder that such and such *daratha*s have been left behind, but what has been achieved is also a *daratha*.

Such drawing attention to the persistence of some form of *daratha* is a rather important aspect of this meditative approach, which from the outset emphasizes oneness and thus a form of tranquil abiding. With the subsequent perceptions to be taken up later, the meditative trajectory can lead to rather sublime and profound experiences. There is therefore quite realistically a danger of latching on to these experiences, rather than using them as tools to proceed further. Their purpose is to liberate, not to create the bondage of attachment.

The situation could be illustrated with food. Although much attention is given to its taste, its real function is to nourish the body. This function should be given prominence. If instead all attention is on the taste, we may end up eating in ways that harm the body rather than giving it the nourishment it needs. In the same way, the function of meditation is to nourish. It can be quite tasty, as is indeed the case for some of the perceptions described here, but the overall purpose should be on providing nourishment. The overarching rationale of this series of perceptions is not to create special experiences—although these almost inevitably result from its implementation—but to reveal the emptiness of *all* experiences. The practice described here is not about getting this attainment or the other, but about cultivating the most thorough letting go possible.

Perhaps awareness of the possibility of becoming intoxicated with the content of meditative perceptions related to emptiness, and thereby failing to see through them, motivated the emphasis on contemplating even the most sublime and profound experience of emptiness as a *daratha*, a disturbance and something to become weary of. In order to facilitate that, even the rather strong connotations of *daratha* are perhaps apposite. That is, even though the term seems too coarse for the subtler parts of the practice to be covered in the next chapters, an intentional employment of such a strong qualification may have seemed required. It can forestall missing out on the overarching purpose of these practices, which is to facilitate insight into the nature of experience, rather than holding on and clinging to the content of any particular experience.

5. Absence

The qualification of being empty draws attention to an absence, and noting what is absent forms a continuous theme in the instructions. This eventually leads to emptiness in its supreme sense, in the form of the complete absence of defilements in the mind to be gained with full awakening. The starting point for this lofty goal is the down-to-earth notion of absence, just as it manifests in the present situation. In the case of the Buddha and Ānanda being at the palace of Migāra's mother, it was directly visible to both that various animals, wealth, and gatherings of people were absent.

The idea of paying attention to what is absent is a recurring one in early Buddhist meditation practice.[45] An example can be found in instructions for contemplation of the mind given in the Discourse on the Establishments of Mindfulness and its parallels. These instructions require being mindfully aware of not only the presence of mental defilements like lust, anger, and delusion but also of the absence of each.[46]

As already noted in the previous chapter, such absence of defilements carries a distinctly positive connotation. This can be seen in another discourse, which reports the physician Jīvaka proclaiming that the Buddha was abiding in *mettā/maitrī*. The Buddha confirms this by stating that all of the root defilements, whereby ill will could arise, have been completely overcome by him.[47] This can be related to the need, proposed in the previous chapter, to base emptiness meditation on a cultivation of *mettā/maitrī* as well as of compassion. The proclamation by Jīvaka provides an additional inspiration for such practice, as it can serve as yet another modality for walking in the footsteps of the Buddha.

These examples bring out positive nuances of absence, thereby countering the perhaps natural tendency to equate absence to some form of lack or deficiency. Presumably due to such negative associations, the mind tends to ignore absence and focuses just on what is present. Yet, the meditative trajectory under discussion here can be taken as an invitation to pay attention to absence as well and thereby perhaps learn to re-evaluate it, divesting it of one-sided connotations of being invariably some form of deficit. This is clearly not the sole connotation absence carries in early Buddhist thought. Alongside expressing that something is lacking, absence can convey something positive.

This holds without doubt for the type of absence that forms the main implication of the perception of the forest as the first step in the gradual approach to emptiness: seclusion in its role of affording the appropriate setting for formal meditation. The positive nature of such absence comes to the fore in a verse, extant in a range of parallels, which highlights the delightful nature of forests for those who are not in search of sensual gratification. Here is a translation of the Pāli version, in the hope that the poem captures at least some of the points to be kept in mind when cultivating the perception of the forest:[48]

> Delightful are forest wilds,
> Where common people do not delight;
> Those free of sensual passion will delight in it,
> Not being in quest of sensual pleasures.

6. Summary

The gradual meditation on emptiness affords an opportunity to walk in the Buddha's footsteps, with its starting point being the present situation right here and now, as it is. The overall trajectory of contemplating the quality of being empty in terms of a specific absence manifests in the case of the present step in the perception of the forest, representative of seclusion. Physical seclusion in terms of the absence of potential disturbances can be complemented by mental seclusion. Overall, the meditative trajectory involves a re-evaluation of absence, clarifying that it need not be invariably negative. The presence of an absence can indeed be the presence of something rather positive and welcome.

A particularly welcome form of absence results from overcoming the five hindrances of sensual desire, anger or ill will, sloth-and-torpor, restlessness-and-worry, and doubt. This type of absence has considerable creative capacity, as it forms the foundation for successful meditation practice. Another helpful quality is contentment, in the form of learning to be equally at ease with both absence and presence. Noting absence can also serve as a useful tool to face various challenges. If one part of the body is sick, for example, attention to the absence of illness in other parts of the body can help broaden perspective and counter the tendency of the mind to narrow down, focus on the afflicted part, and become fully identified with the pain. The same basic strategy can be applied to a range of different situations, in the form of recognizing that things could be worse. In this way, intelligent and creative use of attending to absence has a remarkable potential.

The basic pattern of meditative contemplation, relevant also to subsequent steps, calls for viewing what is absent and what is present. What the present experience is not empty of, what is still there, needs to be recognized as a disturbance or weariness. This qualification can fruitfully be understood to convey the sense of something not yet being the supreme coolness of the final goal. Paying attention to the presence of a disturbance or weariness serves to avoid any clinging to the content of the meditative experience, in order to remain on track for the overall aim of seeing through the nature of all experiences. The transformative dimension of meditation on emptiness is not found just in the successful establishing of the different meditative perceptions themselves. Instead, it involves the eradication of attachment to any experience.

7. Practical Instructions

For formal meditation it would be helpful to find a sitting posture in which the back can be kept straight and the rest of the body relaxed. A helpful preparatory practice is to give the body a little massage in order to bring about relaxation and a balance of bodily energies. This can begin by rubbing the hands against each other to stimulate the energy in the palms, and then place these on the eyelids to relax these, then massage the forehead, scalp, face, and neck, and from there the shoulders, arms, and hands, as well as the torso, legs, and feet. Throughout, the emphasis in the mind is on relaxing and letting go of any tension. Another preparatory practice could be intentional breathing through alternate nostrils in order to balance energy further. This can be done by closing one nostril with the help of a finger and breathing in through the other, then instead closing that nostril and breathing out through the formerly closed nostril. Then breathe in through the same nostril, close it, and breath out through the other. A few cycles of such alternate breathing can help to align energetically the left and right side of the brain in particular and the body in general, thereby further enhancing relaxation.

Keeping the eyes open or closed during sitting meditation is up to individual preferences; in a way, both have their advantages and could be employed in keeping with whatever fits the requirements of our personal meditation practice. Starting off with the actual meditation, the recommendation would be to begin by recalling that this practice is an opportunity to walk in the Buddha's footsteps. The steps in the gradual meditation on emptiness clearly have the purpose of enabling others to emulate the Buddha's own abiding in emptiness. The joy that often quite naturally arises from this reflection can be combined with taking a moment to formulate our own motivation. This motivation could have some relationship to the realization of emptiness, and it should come with a clear altruistic dimension, in the sense of sincerely expressing our compassionate wish that others benefit from our dedication to this meditation session. This in a way already introduces the main theme of absence, here in the sense of absence of selfishness. The Buddha's compassion can serve as an inspiring example for the creative potential of such absence.

With the motivation in place, perception of the forest can be cultivated through an acknowledgment of what is absent in the present situation, thereby affording meditative seclusion. If the mind tends toward distraction, such a survey of what is absent can be done in detail, attending to various things that are absent, in order to keep the mind occupied. If the mind is already calm, however, just a brief reminder of absence will suffice. Next, seclusion in the mental realm can be taken up, by checking in on the actual condition of the mind in order to see if it is overwhelmed by one or the other of the five hindrances. If that is the case, the appropriate antidotes should be employed. Once at least gross manifestations of the five hindrances are absent, it becomes possible to abide in the agreeable condition of the mind that is not hindered by any of these five. Attention given to this pleasurable mental condition of absence can become a subtle source of joy.

From awareness of the absence of disturbances, be these external or internal, practice can proceed by just remaining with a general sense of absence, without going into any further details of what precisely is absent, in order to facilitate the thrust toward oneness mentioned in the Smaller Discourse on Emptiness. The present step is predominantly an introduction to the basic pattern of paying attention to what is absent. With the evolution of the meditative trajectory, to be explored in the subsequent chapters, this first step can become a fairly brief starter, just enough to prepare the terrain for what follows.

Here and with other steps, once the time has come to conclude the session, a counterpart to formulating our motivation would fall into place by sharing our merits, before getting up from the cushion and doing whatever needs to be done next. When engaging in that, and throughout the rest of the day, whenever occasion allows, it can be helpful to note what is absent. In other words, interweaving the theme of absence into daily activities in one way or another would be a welcome complement to the sitting practice. This can take a range of different dimensions. It could take the form of noting that between the eyes and the seen there is space in the form of an absence of visible obstructions. An audible type of absence occurs with moments of silence, even just the short silence between one word and the next. The space afforded by the lack of physical obstructions, enabling movements of the body or walking, is another form of absence. A particularly powerful approach to absence, however, aligns with the daily-life practices surveyed in the previous chapter: the absence of defilements in the mind during any activity or in any bodily posture.

III. Earth

Again, Ānanda, not attending to the perception of people and not attending to the perception of the forest, a monastic attends to oneness in dependence on the perception of earth. Their mind enters upon, is pleased with, settles on, and is devoted to the perception of earth.

Ānanda, it is just like a bull's hide that has been stretched well by a hundred pegs, being free from folds. Ānanda, in the same way, not attending to any highs and lows on this earth, rivers and [places] difficult to ford, places with stumps and thorns, mountains and uneven [places], a monastic attends to oneness in dependence on the perception of earth. Their mind enters upon, is pleased with, settles on, and is devoted to the perception of earth.

They understand like this: "Whatever disturbances there could be in dependence on the perception of people, these are not present here. Whatever disturbances there could be in dependence on the perception of the forest, these are not present here. There is just this remainder of disturbance, namely the oneness in dependence on the perception of earth."

They understand: "This perceptual range is empty of the perception of people"; and they understand: "This perceptual range is empty of the perception of the forest. There is just this non-emptiness, namely the oneness in dependence on the perception of earth."

Thus, they contemplate it as empty of what is indeed not there, and they understand that what remains there is still

> present: "It is there." Ānanda, like this there also comes to be for them this genuine, undistorted, and purified entry into emptiness.[49]

1. The Perception of Earth

The second step in the gradual meditation on emptiness proceeds from the perception of the forest, representative of seclusion, to the perception of earth. The instruction clarifies that the abstract concept of earth is intended, to be arrived at by not paying attention to any irregularities manifesting on the surface of any part of the earth.[50] The image of a bull's hide without any fold, due to being well stretched, conveys the same sense of an abstract notion of earth that does not involve paying attention to any irregularities.

The Pāli commentary relates the present perception to the cultivation of the *kasiṇa* of earth,[51] so that from its perspective executing the present step would involve a visual perception of earth. How far this is indeed the implication of the instructions in the Smaller Discourse on Emptiness requires some exploration. Readers not interested in the technicalities of this topic may prefer to skip what comes next and shift to the sub-header "4. The Elements and Insight" to continue reading (below p. 46).

The Pāli term *kasiṇa* (Sanskrit: *kṛtsna*) stands for a perceptual "totality," gained through the cultivation of concentration on any out of a set of ten objects, one of which is earth. The list of ten objects for such practice comprises the four elements (earth, water, fire, and wind), four colors (blue, yellow, red, and white), space, and consciousness.[52] A Pāli discourse qualifies the meditative experience of each totality as "boundless" (*appamāṇa/apramāṇa*), further specified to involve a cultivation in all directions, above, below, and across. In addition, the same discourse also qualifies each totality as "nondual" (*advaya*).

The qualification "boundless" regularly occurs in relation to the divine abodes (*brahmavihāra*). The specification "nondual" features only rarely in Pāli discourses; in addition to occurring in listings of the ten *kasiṇa*s, it appears to be found in only one other context (where it also occurs together with "boundless"). The relevant passage describes the *mettā/maitrī* cultivated by the Buddha's attendant Ānanda toward his teacher by way of body, speech, and mind, a context where a translation like "undivided" or "wholehearted" would probably capture the intended sense.[53]

The qualification "oneness" in the instructions quoted above implies that the experience of earth should indeed be cultivated as a perceptive totality and thus as a nondual experience, even though the term "nondual" is not explicitly used. At the same time, however, the perception of the forest is similarly described as leading to oneness, even though the forest does not occur among the standard list of *kasiṇas*. In other words, in spite of some similarities, the idea of considering the present passage to be a straightforward case of *kasiṇa* practice is not necessarily compelling.

2. Earth as a *Kasiṇa*

The traditional approach described in the chief manual of Theravāda exegesis for developing the earth *kasiṇa* as a totality focuses on visual apperception. One should fashion a disk covered with earth, taking care to avoid earth of four unsuitable colors (namely those resembling the four colors that serve as alternative *kasiṇas*). Then one gazes at the device and concentrates on it until it becomes possible to see the image of the earth disk in one's mind, without any need to look at the external device. The resultant inner image then becomes the object of concentration. With continued development, it can eventually issue in the attainment of absorption. Due to the emphasis on the visual dimension in Theravāda exegesis, the Pāli term *kasiṇa* has come to denote the visible device fashioned to arouse the initial image of earth, etc.[54]

Adopting the same procedure is not without difficulties when it comes to the two elements of fire and wind, as well as the last two items in the list: space and consciousness. An object of concentration should be stable; hence the moving flames of a fire would not work so well, although this can be remedied by looking at the center of the fire, perhaps through a screen with a hole, thereby facilitating focus on a place that is less affected by motion. Wind, in turn, is nothing but motion and not itself visible, but is only apprehended by the eye when it affects visible objects. In fact, the chief manual of Theravāda exegesis under discussion acknowledges that the element of wind can be apprehended visually or by way of touch.[55] Space is not visible. It also has no visible effect on other objects, nor is it directly touchable, but only manifests in the absence of obstruction to touch. Hence, to turn space into a visible object is only possible by attending to visible absence. But even such strategies would not work with consciousness, which is quite definitely neither a visible nor a tangible object.

The challenges with the last case, which additionally also involves the probably equally challenging dimension of turning the subjective knowing into the object of what is known, may well be why Theravāda exegesis has dropped consciousness from the list and replaced it with the light *kasiṇa*, to be cultivated by attending to sunlight or moonlight shining through a hole.[56] The choice of the light *kasiṇa* may have been influenced by a tendency in some texts to relate the mind to luminosity experienced internally,[57] wherefore focusing on the external luminosity of natural light could have seemed an appropriate substitute for consciousness.

Notably, a chief manual of Sarvāstivāda exegesis has not taken this step and instead presents the same list of ten that is also found in the discourses, including consciousness. The same work reports different opinions on the type of objects to be used for cultivating the ten totalities. One such opinion by some teachers is that the first four in the list—the four elements—have tangibles as their objects, and only the subsequently mentioned four—the four colors—concern visual objects.[58]

It is indeed the case that, even with what looks solid or wet to the eyes, we may at times be uncertain and will then proceed to touch the object in question to make sure. This makes it reasonable to consider earth and water to be more tangible objects than visual ones. The element of fire stands representative for a broad range of temperatures, of which only the extreme of intense heat leads to the visible appearance of flames. Less intense degrees of warmth are often not visible and would thus depend on the sense of touch to be detected. Similarly, the manifestation of wind can at times be so soft that it does not result in easily visible effects, even though it can be sensed through the faculty of touch. In this way, considering the set of four elements—representative of the qualities of solidity, wetness/cohesion, temperature, and motion—as tangible objects would encounter fewer difficulties than taking all of these four to be objects of vision.

3. Earth as Solidity

The upshot of the above, perhaps a bit technical, discussion is an invitation to reconsider the description in the passage translated above: "highs and lows on this earth, rivers and [places] difficult to ford, places with stumps and thorns, mountains and uneven [places]." Although it certainly makes sense to read this as a visual description, it is worthy of note that the description does not mention anything that is only visible, such as a color. This differs from the Theravāda manual, which (as mentioned above) starts off its description of the earth device (= "*kasiṇa*") by stipulating the appropriate color. The description given in the Pāli discourse, however, appears to be more about what a traveler would encounter, such as having to climb highs and lows, crossing rivers and other places difficult to ford, trying to avoid stumbling over stumps and getting hurt by thorns, and needing to get across or around mountains and other uneven places. This is overall more a somatic than just a visual experience.

The same perspective of not necessarily being confined to just the visual dimension could also be extended to the bull's hide, well stretched so that it is without folds. This can be experienced through the eyes but also by touching it, running our hands over the smooth surface created in this way. Since in the ancient setting such a bull's hide would presumably have been used to sit on, given the custom of sitting on the ground, the image of being without folds may even naturally have conveyed a tangible nuance to the audience of the discourse. The Chinese and Tibetan parallels offer an additional illustration, according to which the earth should be seen as similar to the palm of our hand.[59] This additional image would also in principle be open to both proposed interpretations, as the flatness of the palm can be seen but also experienced through the sense of touch.

A shift from a solely visual focus to including the dimension of touch would also accord well with the basic idea of earth as the quality of solidity. Although solidity is usually visible, the most obvious association this quality calls up in the mind is the idea of resistance, and that is a tangible experience. A listing of instances of the earth element found within our own body includes not only easily visible parts like hairs, nails, teeth, and skin but also various inner organs. The Pāli and Chinese versions of such listings agree in summarizing their enumeration of bodily parts to be concerned with whatever is found within our body and is solid.[60] What the different parts of our own body share in common is indeed such solidity in the sense of resistance to touch.

As a side note to this list of bodily parts, the implication is not that anatomical parts like nails and teeth are solely earth element. Another discourse clarifies that a log of wood contains each of the four elements.[61] In other words, even though a log of wood or the nails and teeth of a human body can serve as self-evident exemplifications of the principle of solidity, each of these also contains the other three elements, albeit to a lesser degree. Anything solid will contain some degree of cohesion (= water), have some temperature (= fire), and be pervaded by some inner motion (= wind).

In relation to the instructions given at the outset of this chapter, due to the intrinsic interrelationship among the four elements, a reference to earth implicitly covers also the other three elements. Although the emphasis is on earth as representative of solidity, it stands to reason to include the contribution made by the other elements to that very experience of solidity, a topic I will explore from a practice-related perspective in relation to the meditative progression from earth to infinite space.

4. The Elements and Insight

Besides featuring as possible objects for the cultivation of concentration, the four elements also have a prominent role to play in relation to insight. The detailed instructions on mindfulness in the *Satipaṭṭhānasutta* and its parallels dedicate one of their body contemplations to awareness of the elements within the human body. The gist of this exercise finds exemplification in a simile, which describes a butcher who has just cut up a cow.[62] The Pāli commentary explains that the simile points to a shift in perspective from "cow" to various pieces of "meat."[63] In the same way, by contemplating the elements, a meditator can experience a shift of perspective from mistaking the body to be a substantial entity to seeing it just as a combination of qualities, namely the four qualities represented by the four elements.

The butcher simile shows the thrust of this practice to be toward insight into the empty nature of material phenomena. This is in line with the attitude toward the material elements by someone who has reached the final goal of liberation: an arahant (Sanskrit: *arhat*) is completely free from any self-notion or appropriation in regard to the earth element or any of the other elements.[64] The idea of endowing the earth or any other element with the status of being ultimately real is a later development. In the early discourses, earth and other elements feature as mere qualities. These are empty of some sort of intrinsic essence, being the product of conditions through and through.

The conditionality of the elements is already to some extent implicit in the circumstance that they occur together, rather than in isolation. This perspective holds even at the level of ancient Indian cosmology, evident in an explanation of what was believed to be one of the causes for the occurrence of an earthquake. The explanation proposes that the Earth rests on water, water rests on wind, and wind on space.[65] Hence, when winds blow in space, the water gets agitated, and that in turn leads to an earthquake. Although the fire element does not come up explicitly in this context, another discourse, extant in a range of parallels, describes a future increase in solar heat—illustrated with the depiction of up to seven suns arising one after the other—as a result of which even the highest mountain on the Earth will be completely burned up.[66] This scenario implies that it is thanks to the limited amount of solar heat produced by the present sun that the Earth with its various mountains continues to exist for the time being.

The same perspective can be applied to the human body. The solidity of the body depends on the principle of cohesion. If the body were to be completely without water, it would dry up and fall apart, no longer being able to function. It also needs to be at the right temperature. The increase in solar heat that in the future is expected to burn up even mountains would certainly render the existence of human bodies impossible. The same holds for a lesser degree of heat; in fact, the human body can only survive within a relatively narrow temperature range. If directly exposed for some time to anything above or below that temperature range, the body will become dysfunctional and succumb to death. Motion is also needed; in fact, without the continuous minor motions inside the body or without even the motion of air coming in and going out, the body would not remain alive, and its solidity would disintegrate during the process of decomposition that sets in once the body has breathed its last. It is only due to the appropriate contribution made by the other three elements that the human body continues to live and remain solid rather than fall apart. In this way, be it the external or the internal earth element, both depend on the other elements for their very existence. It follows that the earth element is indeed empty, being nothing but a product of a combination of conditions.

5. Tranquility and Insight

The two dimensions of the earth element, which emerged during the above survey, can be related to a topic that is of considerable relevance to the entire meditative approach to emptiness examined here, namely tranquility and insight. Like the case of the four elements, in early Buddhist thought tranquility and insight are predominantly qualities, rather than designating strictly separate compartments of meditation practice. Moreover, there is no definite sequence to be followed in their cultivation, as we may develop tranquility first and then insight, or else insight first and then tranquility, or else we may cultivate both in conjunction.[67]

The present discourse on emptiness appears to furnish a good example of such flexible interrelation of tranquility and insight. This becomes particularly evident with the perceptions of infinite space, infinite consciousness, and nothingness, to be taken up subsequent to the perception of earth. These three perceptions are taken from the realm of tranquility, where they feature as the themes taken by the first three immaterial spheres. In the present setting, however, these perceptions instead serve the purpose of cultivating insight into emptiness. The obverse can be seen in another discourse, similarly extant in Pāli, Chinese, and Tibetan, which employs insight contemplations in order to cultivate tranquility attainments, a topic to which I will return in a subsequent chapter (see below p. 98).[68]

For an appreciation of the instructions translated above, the possibility of such an interrelation between tranquility and insight is of considerable relevance, as it helps to combine the recurrent reference to oneness with the equally recurrent instruction to notice what is absent and what is present, in terms of disturbances and emptiness. The mode of practice that emerges from such instructions can indeed be considered a conjunction of tranquility and insight. In practical terms, each individual meditator can decide which of these two qualities should be given prominence in the present situation, under the overarching aim of cultivating both in tandem. At times, emphasis can just be on abiding in the unitary nature of the respective perception, giving room to a deepening of tranquility. At other times, more emphasis can be on comprehending what the particular perception implies, thereby actualizing its insight potential.

In the present case, then, the growth of tranquility can take the form of resting in a unitary experience of earth, whenever this seems appropriate. If instead the actual condition of the mind calls for a more engaging mode of practice, the alternative option of insight cultivation would fall into place by way of letting the implications of the perception of earth sink into the mind and effect a transformation of our inner attitude and evaluations. In addition to the disturbances already left behind with the perception of the forest, the disturbances left behind with the perception of the earth are the alienation and fragmentation that result from excessive individualism, a tendency particularly prominent in contemporary Westernized societies. In countering this tendency, perception of earth points to the individual's interrelatedness with other life on this planet, providing a grounding in reality and a sense of overall belonging.

In order to avoid potential misunderstandings, it may be of use to clarify that opening up this perspective does not in any way intend to impose some sort of norm or imply even a trace of disregard for the rights of the individual. As evident in the instruction translated at the outset of this chapter, the rivers, mountains, stumps, and thorns are simply seen as they individually manifest. The instruction is not to dry up the rivers, level the mountains, dig out the stumps, or cut down the thorns. These are left just the way they are. But the perception to be cultivated sees them as part of something larger; it invites a zooming out from the tendency of attention to focus on one thing at the expense of the rest and instead encourages taking in the whole picture. As a result, a taste of underlying unity can pervade experience.

In terms of the previous perception of the forest, the perception of earth can counterbalance excessive emphasis on what affords seclusion. It is reasonable to try to establish whatever degree of seclusion seems possible in order to meditate. At the same time, however, it is perhaps even more important not to become obsessive about the proper conditions for meditation. Here, the basic interrelatedness with others that comes with the perception of earth can help to restore balance whenever it has been lost. In the face of whatever disturbances may manifest, internally or externally, the meditator can stay grounded and firm, like a mountain rooted in the ground. This brings out an important dimension of emptiness practice and at the same time can be taken as a convenient summary of central aspects of the present perception: the ability to remain unshaken among the ups and downs of life. Here is a poem that conveys a key aspect of such practice with the image of a solid rock unshaken by winds:[69]

> Like a solid rock
> Is not moved by the wind,
> So the wise are not moved
> Amid blame and praise.

6. Summary

The perception of earth, mentioned in the instructions in the Smaller Discourse on Emptiness, concerns the abstract notion of earth. The cultivation of this abstract notion leads to an experience of oneness in the form of a perceptual totality. In spite of some similarities, it remains doubtful whether the instructions intend the *kasiṇa* of earth, as assumed by the commentary. In particular, it does not seem necessary to confine the present instructions to a visual apperception of the earth. Instead, it is reasonable to allow for the alternative approach of sensing earth as solidity through the faculty of bodily touch.

As the first of the four elements, earth implicitly includes the other three. Although the instructions are just about the earth element, whose role is to lead over from the previous perception of the forest to the subsequent perception of infinite space, in an implicit manner the other three elements can be considered as playing a secondary role. Be it the earth element outside or its manifestations inside of the body, any such manifestation depends on the other elements. The earth element depends on cohesion for being solid; water depends on warmth for cohesion; fire depends on motion for being warm. Contemplating in this way, the empty and insubstantial nature of the body—as well as of any external manifestation of the element earth—can become a palpable, personal, and direct experience.

The above shows that, besides their potential for the development of the meditative quality of tranquility, the four elements also have considerable potential in relation to the growth of insight. This holds in particular for discerning the empty nature of anything material. A close interrelation of the qualities of tranquility and insight is indeed a continuous feature of the gradual meditative entry into emptiness, where an encouragement to abide in meditative oneness combines with an emphasis on seeing the respective disturbance or weariness, whereby the emptiness of what is absent comes with an acknowledgment of the non-emptiness of what is still present. The two dimensions that emerge in this way can be taken as an invitation to adjust the practice flexibly, according to what the present moment and personal conditions seem to require, under the overarching aim of a balanced cultivation of both tranquility and insight.

7. Practical Instructions

Implementing the present step takes off from the preceding one described in the previous chapter regarding the perception of the forest: at first we formulated our motivation and then practice proceeded from attending to external absence and internal absence to the abstract notion of absence as such, based on a mind that is free from the hindrances.

Perception of earth as solidity can then conveniently be developed based on a body scan. Although the procedure of scanning the body is not explicitly found in the early discourses,[70] it provides an expedient means for rooting awareness in the whole body and at the same time making the notion of solidity easier to experience.

Perhaps the present occasion of recommending the body scan is a good opportunity for me to clarify my overall position: The instructions here and elsewhere do not come with the least pretense at being the only right way or being a definite reflection of how meditation on emptiness was done at the time of the Buddha. Instead, within the limits of my understanding and abilities, I try to present an approach that does justice to what I believe the instructions translated at the outset of each chapter convey, which in turn are contextualized with what comparative study of the Chinese and Tibetan parallel suggests. Hence, the invitation is simply to try out what I present and see if it works.

With this much clarified, the idea of employing a body scan to develop a tangible experience of the earth element does not require cultivating sensitivity to solidity in each and every part of the body. The point is only to use the body scan as an approach for becoming conscious of solidity being present in the body, without being too concerned about to what extent such an awareness is conceptual or a directly felt experience. Rather than being two opposite modalities of contemplation, the conceptual input and the direct experience can preferably be seen as part of a continuum, which allows a whole range of different combinations of the two. Even the most direct experience of earth will still involve a minimum of concepts, otherwise we would not know what we are experiencing, and even the most conceptual notion of earth will still be part of our own present experience. Although the distinction between these two may be important in meditation traditions that draw a sharp divide between tranquility and insight, the early Buddhist approach to contemplation of emptiness combines these two and therefore can afford the freedom of not needing to problematize the judicious employment of concepts or assuming that there is a need to break through to some form of unmediated, direct experience. Instead, similar to learning any task, such as playing a musical instrument, there is an initial period of apprenticeship during which more concepts are required. With growing familiarity and expertise, these will become fewer and fewer, leaving room for the eventual occurrence of a flow-like experience in performing the music as well as when abiding in meditation.

Actual practice can start with the top of the head, simply becoming aware of that part of the body in the knowledge that there is solidity. From the top of the head, attention can shift to the whole head, and from there to the neck, both shoulders simultaneously, the arms, and the hands, each time simply becoming aware of that part of the body, being mindfully present to it, in the knowledge that there is some solidity there. Continuing with the same procedure, attention can turn to the torso, the entire pelvis, the legs, and the feet. If for some reason the proposed sequence of bodily parts does not work so well, meditators should feel free to change to a different sequence that works better for them.

The completion of the scan can then lead on to being aware of the whole body in the meditation posture as being pervaded by the element of earth, by solidity. This can be enhanced by becoming aware of the experience of gravity as a subtle sense of pulling the body downward. Such a strengthening of the experience of solidity of the whole body through feeling the pull of gravity can be combined with letting go of any tension or distracting thoughts, just allowing these to sink into the ground and disappear.

Next, attention can turn to the parts of the body that touch the ground, and from there awareness can explore the external earth. From the area that can be felt directly, practice can proceed by enlarging the perception of the ground, zooming out as it were, from the environment close by to the region, state, continent, and eventually the whole planet Earth. This can lead to a sense of the body being seated on the planet Earth, in awareness of the intimate connection between the former and the latter, of the oneness of the internal and external earth element. Directly evidenced by the sense of gravity that keeps the body grounded, the planet Earth provides support for the body, including food, water, and above all a continuous supply of oxygen produced by its plants, which enable the body to breathe and stay alive.

In order to strengthen the sense of belonging and grounding in the Earth, soft awareness of the process of breathing can accompany the whole-body awareness. As mentioned earlier, it is preferable not to focus on the breath at the exclusion of everything else. Instead of focusing, the idea is to foreground mindfulness of the whole body in the meditation posture and then experience the process of breathing, the alternation between inhalations and exhalations, as an integral part of such whole-body awareness. The body as a whole stays connected to the ground and through that to the whole planet Earth, connected by way of the sense of gravity, and also connected through a continuous exchange with the outer environment by way of inhaling and exhaling. To repeat, the process of breathing is experienced in the periphery of the field of attention, rather than being at its center. It features as just another dimension of whole-body awareness, similar to, and alongside with, the sense of gravity.

If it has been possible to establish such soft and peripheral awareness of the process of breathing, then the natural rhythm provided by the alternation between inhalations and exhalations can be employed as a means to facilitate remaining in the present moment, similar to the mode of practice suggested earlier for the divine abodes (see above p. 22). Alongside each inhalation, a bit more emphasis could be given to the experience of the internal earth element, the solidity of the body in the meditation posture. With every exhalation, a bit more emphasis could be given to the experience of the external earth element, the solidity of the planet Earth as the ground that supports the body.

The perception of earth, established in this way, can be of considerable help to step out of the unnecessary creation of dualistic contrasts. Instead of being completely lost in the distinction between what is beautiful and ugly, for example, such evaluations can be seen as parts of the same continuum. The notion of beauty requires the notion of ugliness; the one cannot exist without the other. The idea need not be to throw out such notions altogether but only to soften their edges and to find ease in the awareness of what these and other apparent contrasts concerning material phenomena share in common. The differences that exist between one manifestation of materiality and another do not really deserve the amount of importance we usually attribute to them. Undertaken in this way, the perception of earth can help to strike at the root of conceit within, at the tendency to measure ourselves in comparison with others based on the attractiveness or ability of our own body. It can introduce a healthy degree of balance, combined with the understanding that all bodies, however they may appear, are just manifestations of the earth element and share with our own body that they are supported and maintained continuously by the Earth.

Having rested in this experience of the element earth for however long it may seem appropriate, a step in preparation for the transition to the next perception of infinite space, to be explored in the next chapter, would then be to bring in the other three elements. In terms of the present perception, bringing in the other three elements serves to ensure that the nature of the earth element is fully understood for what it is. This can again be done through body scans. Beginning with the area where the body touches the ground as an exemplification of cohesion, awareness can move from the feet upward to the legs, pelvis, torso, hands, arms, shoulders, neck, and head, in the awareness that all of these bodily parts are pervaded by some degree of the water element, which provides their cohesion. Again, there is no need to strain to feel that directly. It is perfectly fine just to move through the parts of the body and know, conceptually, that there must be some degree of water element in the form of wetness and cohesion. Awareness of the whole body as pervaded by the water element can then combine with the understanding that the very solidity of the body relies on the cohesion provided by the water element.

An exploration of the fire element can in turn conveniently begin with the head, so that each body scan continues from the place where the previous one has concluded. Perhaps the facial area may be a good starting point for feeling the difference between the outside temperature and the temperature inside of the body, or alternatively perhaps the difference between inhalations and exhalations could be noted, the former usually being just a bit cooler than the latter. Or else just the conceptual idea of fire as warmth and temperature can be relied on to start the body scan from the head downward to the neck, shoulders, arms, hands, torso, pelvis, legs, and feet. Awareness of the whole body as pervaded by the fire element can combine with the understanding of the need for the fire element, by way of providing the appropriate temperature, to support the water element in its function of facilitating the body's solidity.

The area where the body touches the ground naturally stimulates some sensations, which could be just a general sense of pressure. However, on closer inspection at times some other sensations can be noted, perhaps some tingling or throbbing, pulsating of blood, itching, or anything else that is of a palpably changing nature. All these are manifestations of motion, the wind element. In the understanding that such motion occurs throughout the body—and without attempting to feel that distinctly in each and every part of the body—the scan can proceed upward from the feet to the legs, pelvis, torso, hands, arms, shoulders, neck, and head, each time being aware of the presence of some degree of wind element in the respective part of the body. This can lead to awareness of the whole body in the meditation posture, experienced from the viewpoint of the wind element—that is, from the viewpoint of the various motions that take place inside of it. Fire is but a manifestation of motion; hence the present step can combine with the understanding of the need for the wind element as the basic principle required for fire to exist, thereby completing the understanding of the dependency of the four elements on each other. Out of the various motions that take place in the body, the ingoing breaths and the outgoing breaths are particularly indispensable for it to maintain its solidity as a living body, for it to continue being alive. This understanding can be related to peripheral awareness of the process of breathing as a dimension of the experience of the seated body viewed from the perspective of its inner motions.

Having rested in this experience for as long as may seem suitable, the time may have come to conclude the meditation session. Here as well as with subsequent perceptions, it can be quite helpful to proceed briefly through the same steps in a backward order. In the present case, this could be implemented without going through another detailed body scan and instead just by becoming aware of the body as earth element and then calling up again the perception of the forest, seclusion within and without. Sharing our merits can provide the appropriate concluding point for the meditation session.

In terms of its application to daily-life situations, whole-body awareness combined with attending to the sense of gravity that connects the body to the earth can be a very useful tool to enable staying grounded in any situation, in line with the image in the poem quoted above regarding becoming like a solid rock that is unshaken by winds. Another example for implementing the perception of earth would be partaking of food, which usually is evaluated as delicious or unsavory. A monastic practice that can be quite revealing in this respect is to put all the food into a single dish or container and then to mix it. The nourishing of the body remains the same, but the excitement of the taste buds is substantially diminished, and a perception of sameness arises. Cultivating the perception of sameness in this or any other way can go a long way toward undermining the tendency to dramatize dualistic evaluations and learning to take them less seriously.

IV. Infinite Space

Again, Ānanda, not attending to the perception of the forest and not attending to the perception of earth, a monastic attends to oneness in dependence on the perception of the sphere of infinite space. Their mind enters upon, is pleased with, settles on, and is devoted to the perception of the sphere of infinite space.

They understand like this: "Whatever disturbances there could be in dependence on the perception of the forest, these are not present here. Whatever disturbances there could be in dependence on the perception of earth, these are not present here. There is just this remainder of disturbance, namely the oneness in dependence on the perception of the sphere of infinite space."

They understand: "This perceptual range is empty of the perception of the forest"; and they understand: "This perceptual range is empty of the perception of earth. There is just this non-emptiness, namely the oneness in dependence on the perception of the sphere of infinite space."

Thus, they contemplate it as empty of what is indeed not there, and they understand that what remains there is still present: "It is there." Ānanda, like this there also comes to be for them this genuine, undistorted, and purified entry into emptiness.[71]

1. The Perception of Space

Infinite space is the object of the first of the four immaterial spheres, the other three being infinite consciousness, nothingness, and neither-perception-nor-nonperception, each of which builds on having successfully mastered the previously mentioned immaterial sphere(s). The immaterial sphere of infinite space in turn appears to require mastery of the four absorptions. This is evident from listings of the four absorptions and the four immaterial spheres in a description of successive meditative abidings found in Pāli discourses and their parallels.[72] The implication is that each item in the list requires previous attainment of the items mentioned earlier, which in the case of the immaterial sphere of infinite space are the four absorptions. The same can also be seen in a discourse extant in Pāli and Chinese that presents the fourth absorption as transcending the third (just as this transcends the second and the second transcends the first) and then the attainment of the sphere of infinite space as transcending the fourth absorption.[73] Thus, just as attaining the fourth absorption would require the ability to attain the third, so attaining the sphere of infinite space would require the ability to attain the fourth absorption.

Mastery of the absorptions or any of the immaterial spheres also stands in relation to early Buddhist cosmology, in that each such attainment leads to rebirth in the corresponding realms. In the case of mastery of the sphere of infinite space, a Pāli discourse indicates that the lifespan of those reborn accordingly is twenty thousand eons.[74] An eon corresponds to the time it would take to wear down a solid mountain several miles high by stroking it with a piece of cloth once every hundred years.[75] It follows that a lifespan of twenty thousand eons stands for an incredibly long period of time.

The implications of the concentrative requirement for gaining mastery of the immaterial sphere of infinite space and its lofty rebirth prospects depend on assessing the nature of the fourth absorption. Contrary to a popular trend of presenting the four absorptions as something within easy reach of the average practitioner, a close comparative study of relevant passages in the early discourses conveys the impression that absorption attainment requires considerable meditative mastery.[76] Hence, the ability to attain the fourth absorption at will would be a matter of having acquired a high degree of expertise in concentration.

Nevertheless, a meditative cultivation of the notion of infinite space as such does not require that much, as is evident from its inclusion in the list of *kasiṇas* discussed in the previous chapter (see above p. 42). These are means to cultivate concentration in order to gain absorption and thus obviously can take place at levels of concentration that fall short of even the first absorption. A cultivation of the notion of space in a way that does not rely on previous absorption attainment appears to be indeed the perspective relevant to the passage translated above. Its formulation differs from the way the early discourses usually introduce the attainment of the sphere of infinite space. When referring to the sphere of infinite space, the present instruction does not indicate that one "abides in its attainment" (*upasampajja viharati*) but just that one has the corresponding "perception" (*saññā*). The Chinese and Tibetan versions agree in speaking just of having the "perception" (*xiǎng/'du shes*).[77] Arousing just the perception does not need previously developed absorption ability. It follows that such abilities would not be required in order to be able to execute the instructions given above. What does seem necessary is the absence of distraction to enable maintaining the perception of the sphere of infinite space. This much can be achieved through well-established mindfulness and dedicated practice.

Nevertheless, cultivating the perception of infinite space does require considerable meditative training, especially if we have not yet developed familiarity with leading the mind into a calm abiding without relying on a specific circumscribed focus, such as is possible through the boundless radiation of the divine abodes. For this reason, arousing and maintaining the perception of infinite space may at first subjectively appear challenging and for some time seem to be just an abstract concept. It needs time and dedication until the mind "enters upon, is pleased with, settles on, and is devoted to it," terms that clearly point to the need for mental tranquility.

A cultivation of the perception of infinite space in formal meditation can benefit considerably from experimenting with the perception of space outside of formal meditation. An ideal occasion for doing that could take advantage of being in an open space on a cloudless day. Positioning the body in as relaxed a manner as possible, perhaps even reclining or leaning back in a comfortable chair, we simply gaze at the sky in awareness of its infinite nature. However far the gaze reaches, it is not possible to find any limit to space. Such experimenting with the visual apperception of space in the sky can help us to arouse more easily the meditative notion of infinite space in formal meditation.

Another helpful tool for facilitating formal meditation can take the form of countering possible negative associations with space as being a mere absence. A simile found in a Pāli discourse and its Chinese parallel illustrates the nature of the body with the example of a house.[78] Just as a house consists of space enclosed by building material, so the human body consists of space enclosed by skin, flesh, and bones. Although this is not the explicit purpose of the simile, in both cases the image shows that the respective space has an important function to fulfill. It is the space of the house that can be inhabited, not the building material. Even though we would normally be inclined to give all importance to the building material, on reflection it becomes clear that the space inside the house carries considerable importance. The same holds in turn for the human body. Here, too, we may tend to give all importance to the different organs. Yet, without the space to breathe in or to take in nourishment, the body could not function. Moreover, the greater part of human sensory experience depends on space and not just, as we may unthinkingly assume, on the functionality of the respective sense organs. If the space in front of the eyes is blocked, no seeing will be possible. If the space in the apertures of the ears, the nose, and the mouth is obstructed, hearing, smelling, and tasting will also not be possible, however much the senses themselves are functional. Reflecting along these lines can help to reveal the importance and also the enabling potential of space as that which facilitates a range of activities and events. Clearly, space is not just a blank nothing.

Another avenue for easing into the perception of infinite space can be the cultivation of the four divine abodes. When a boundless abiding in the divine abodes has been practiced, there is already a solid degree of familiarity with space as the field that is pervaded by each *brahmavihāra*, wherefore the perception of infinite space becomes considerably less challenging. This undermines a possible tendency in the mind of wanting to construct space, to make it happen in some way. For this reason, if the perception of infinite space should prove difficult, it can be helpful to dedicate time to a systematic development of all four divine abodes and, after familiarity with these has been achieved, to take boundless abiding in equanimity as the point of transition for attempting again to abide in the perception of infinite space.

2. A Mind like Space

A more reflective employment of the notion of space that does not require absorptive abilities can be seen in an instruction on cultivating a mind like space. Such an instruction forms part of a detailed teaching reportedly given by the Buddha to his son, Rāhula. After covering the four elements and the element of space in their internal and external manifestations, the instruction proceeds by encouraging Rāhula to take inspiration from each of these five elements for cultivating a beneficial mental attitude. The part relevant to space proceeds as follows:

> Rāhula, just like space, which is not established anywhere, in the same way, Rāhula, you should cultivate meditation that is like space. Rāhula, on cultivating meditation that is indeed like space, arisen agreeable and disagreeable contacts will not remain and overwhelm the mind.[79]

The idea of being able to handle the arising of what is agreeable and disagreeable without becoming overwhelmed could be fleshed out with the help of another Pāli discourse, which in agreement with its Chinese parallel describes how to undertake a cultivation of the sense faculties (*indriyabhāvanā*).[80] Accomplishment in such practice leads to establishing equanimity at any sense door, with the understanding that whatever arises is conditioned and coarse, whereas equanimity is peaceful. When the eyes see something agreeable or disagreeable, for example, equanimity can in this way become established as swiftly as someone may close or open their eyes. With sounds that are agreeable or disagreeable, the same ability to establish equanimity is comparable to snapping the fingers; with odors it compares to a raindrop rolling off a sloping lotus leaf (which has a superhydrophobic surface and thus is waterproof, wherefore a drop of rain just rolls off); with flavors it is like spitting out a ball of spittle on the tip of the tongue; with tangibles it is like bending an extended arm or extending a bent arm; and with mental objects it is like a few drops of water that land on a thoroughly heated iron plate and evaporate on the spot.[81]

The powerful images provided by this discourse can be of considerable help in actual practice, showing the ease and swiftness with which reactivity to what is agreeable or disagreeable can be avoided. Needless to say, this is a more advanced practice that would build on previous working with defilements by way of relying on antidotes. Such employment of antidotes to particular defilements clearly has its place, but it need not be seen as the only option. Based on some proficiency in the approach of employing antidotes and the resultant familiarity with our own mental tendencies, at times it becomes possible to deal with reactivity in the mind as swiftly and effortlessly as envisaged in these illustrations.

The understanding that something is conditioned and coarse in contrast to the peaceful nature of equanimity could in principle also be cultivated through the instruction given to Rāhula. The basic task would be to keep the mind like space when anything arises at a sense door. The open receptivity of the space-like mind naturally forestalls the onset of reactivity toward what is being experienced, which necessitates a narrow state of mind focused on likes and dislikes. In contrast, although we still clearly notice the initial impact of what is agreeable and disagreeable, the spaciousness of the mind simply allows this to arise and pass away without being turned into another act in the drama of experience. In terms of the terminology employed in the instruction to Rāhula, the agreeable and the disagreeable will not remain and overwhelm the mind.

Cultivating equanimity through maintaining a mind like space is not some form of escapism by way of turning a blind eye to what is happening. Instead, the mind that is like space is simply too vast to be overwhelmed by the pettiness of any contact through the six senses. The vastness of space puts things into a wider context; it thereby helps forestall reactions stemming from taking whatever happens too personally and then feeling a need to react, which usually leads to the thriving of defilements. Due to the open receptivity of the mind that is like space, there is certainly plenty of room for deciding to take action whenever this is required. However, the decisive difference is that such action springs from deliberation rather than being a compulsive reaction due to feeling overwhelmed.

The same approach applies not only to seeing but of course also to the other senses, including the mind. The agreeable and the disagreeable in the mind can quickly evaporate like water drops falling on a thoroughly heated iron pan. With sufficient training, this approach can be put to good use in relation to thinking activity in general. With a mind that is like space, there is no need to fight thoughts and force the mind into stillness. This is not to devalue thought-free stillness of the mind, but much rather to propose a different approach for arriving at it. Rather than trying to suppress thinking activity, it can simply be noticed as occurring in the vast space of the mind. When thoughts are surrounded by space, as it were, they lose much of their presumed importance and therewith much of their ability to overpower the mind and carry it away. Said differently, arrival at stillness does not require a total absence of thinking activity. Instead, it requires not taking thinking activity so very personally, not identifying with it. When cultivated in this way, the notion of space can become a powerful tool for actualizing the potential of emptiness meditation in relation to the perennial challenge of a distracted mind.

3. No Painting on Space

Working with a distracted mind from the viewpoint of the notion of space can rely on a simile found in another and unrelated discourse extant in Pāli and Chinese. The relevant passage illustrates the impossibility of agitating a well-developed mind with several examples, one of which is the attempt to paint with colors on empty space.[82] Just as space will not be affected by any attempt to paint on it, in the same way one should remain unaffected by any type of disagreeable speech. Both versions conclude the advice by recommending that one should "abide with a space-like mind," adding that such a mind should be developed in a boundless manner so that it pervades the whole world.[83]

An apparent implementation of this imagery can be seen in two consecutive verses seemingly spoken by a monastic in reply to some temptation. The first verse illustrates the vanity of such attempts with the image of trying in vain to paint with colors on empty space, followed by clarifying in the second verse that the speaker had a space-like mind, being inwardly concentrated.[84] In a similar way, challenges of various types can be successfully met with the help of keeping the mind like space.

The idea of coloration can in turn be related to the predicament of the mind being under the influence of sensual desire, the first of the five hindrances. The effect of each hindrance finds illustration in the example of looking at a bowl of water in order to gain an accurate reflection of our own face. A mind under the influence of sensual desire compares to the water in the bowl being colored, as a result of which its surface will not accurately reflect the present condition of our own face.[85] The same inability to reflect accurately what is there holds for the other hindrances: anger compares to boiling water, sloth-and-torpor to it being covered by algae, restlessness-and-worry can have an effect like wind agitating the surface of the water, and doubt resembles the bowl of water being placed in the dark. In each case, the bowl of water will no longer provide an accurate reflection of what is in front of its surface.

These evocative illustrations could be applied to the idea of a space-like mind, whereby any such repercussion will not have scope to take place. Although this is not stated in the original, the hindrance of sensual desire will indeed be unable to color space, which can also not be caused to boil in anger. Space cannot be covered by the slimy algae of sloth-and-torpor or agitated by the wind of restlessness-and-worry, and its nature will also remain unaffected by the darkness of doubt. The point of the proposed application of this set of similes is to convey that the hindrances, particularly when they are weak or just arising, can be summarily dismissed by relying on the space-like mind.

Just to repeat a point made already above, this suggestion is not meant to deny the appropriateness of actively countering the hindrances through antidotes. Working with antidotes certainly has its place when inner seclusion is lacking, in order to establish the appropriate conditions for embarking on emptiness meditation (see above p. 28). However, such active measures are not the only option available. This holds especially if, at a time when emptiness meditation is already well under way, a hindrance should emerge. The space-like mind can provide an appropriate tool when a distraction occurs mid-practice. Since due to the previous trajectory of meditating on emptiness such manifestation of a hindrance or distraction will probably be of the weaker type, it may well be appropriate to opt for the alternative and less energy- and time-consuming approach: the space-like mind.

4. An Unestablished Mind

The powerful instruction to Rāhula, quoted above, qualifies space as "not established." This qualification is quite relevant to the present step in contemplation of emptiness, where with the transition from earth to infinite space the condition of not being established anywhere becomes a prominent characteristic of the meditative experience. Inspiration for such practice can be gained from the circumstance that Nirvana itself is also qualified as "not established."[86] Moreover, arahants and those on the brink of reaching full awakening have a consciousness that is "unestablished."[87] Needless to say, space is not Nirvana and a space-like mind does not mean that one is awakened. Nevertheless, the nuance of not being established points in the direction of Nirvana and awakening, and it is precisely this nuance that marks the difference between the present meditative step and the preceding ones, concerned with the perceptions of the forest and of earth.

As a side note on the preceding trajectory, the reference to the perception of the forest in the instruction for proceeding from the perception of earth to the perception of the sphere of infinite space conforms to a recurrent pattern in the instructions. From a practical perspective, one would think that it suffices to mention just the perception that is indeed being left behind, which in the present case is the perception of earth. Why also mention the previous one, which has already been left behind? At the same time, however, just leaving behind the perception of earth would also apply to reverting to the previous perception of the forest. So perhaps the additional mention of the preceding step serves to make it clear that the leaving behind of the perception of earth at the present juncture of practice should lead onward to the perception of infinite space, in order to continue with the overall momentum of the gradually deepening entry into emptiness.

In principle, it would indeed be possible to proceed through the same series of meditative perceptions in the reverse order. An inspiring example for such a procedure is the report of the Buddha's own last meditation, when on the eve of his passing away he successively attained the four absorptions, the four immaterial spheres, and then cessation, followed by proceeding through the same series in backward order until reaching again his starting point in the first absorption.[88] The same basic pattern can be of considerable practical relevance to the present meditation on emptiness, even though this is not explicitly mentioned in the instructions. If we proceed even just swiftly in the reverse order to return to the starting point in the perception of the forest, then this provides a way of smoothing the transition to daily-life activities and at the same time also helps to deepen appreciation of the insight dimensions of each step. This holds in particular for the disturbance or weariness left behind with each step, as on proceeding in backward order these inevitably increase and are for this reason more easily and clearly discerned. The resultant improved understanding can then inform future instances of cultivating the steps of the gradual meditation on emptiness again in forward order.

With progress to the perception of infinite space achieved, the mind is no longer established on the material side of existence, due to which a whole host of potential disturbances have been left behind. In fact, the standard description of the fully fledged attainment of infinite space explicitly mentions the overcoming of perceptions of "resistance" (Pāli: *paṭigha*; Sanskrit: *pratigha*), which is precisely how we usually experience materiality.

So much excitement and unnecessary suffering has its root in wanting to possess material things. Whole wars with all their horrible consequences are fought for the possession of a bit more territory, a bit more earth. Ownership of material things is the key drive behind a worldwide system of ruthless exploitation that favors the few at the expense of the suffering of the many. Stepping out of the misconception underpinning all this is such a powerful and deeply meaningful thing to do.

At the same time, however, the idea of leaving behind materiality needs to be taken for what it is, namely a meditative strategy and not a statement of an absolute truth. Even after many hours of cultivating the present perception, it will not be possible to walk through a wall. Nor does a cultivation of emptiness meditation on its own suffice for addressing the ills of the world. There is a need to be aware of the limitations of these perceptions, which are just tools for exploring particular ways of viewing experience. These steps in the gradual meditation on emptiness are soteriological strategies and not ontological claims. They are invitations to look at things in a certain way.

According to the early discourses, materiality depends on the four elements and thus not just on the mind.[89] The point of the meditation discussed here is not to pretend that matter is a mere creation of the mind. At the same time, however, the subjective experience of matter is indeed to a substantial degree the creation of our own mind. This contribution to the construction of our own world of experience, made unknowingly by us, is precisely what the whole trajectory of emptiness meditation can gradually reveal. The key aspect for tapping the liberating potential of the perception of infinite space as a step in the gradual meditation on emptiness is the understanding of what it implies. This calls for recognizing what type of disturbance or weariness has been left behind. In the present case, the unified perception of infinite space leaves behind the disturbances that can arise with materiality. At this stage, matter no longer matters.

Although an understanding of what has been left behind can at first be cultivated with the help of intentional reflection, eventually this type of insight will inform the meditative experience in a way that does not involve the intentional employment of conceptual thinking. As a way of gradually building up to that, it can be helpful to bring in reflections on the disturbances left behind whenever the mind is about to lose its composure and just begins to drift away. With mindfulness well established, it becomes possible to notice swiftly when the mind loses the breadth it has had so far through taking an infinite object, which in the present case is the sphere of infinite space, as well as through a gradual diminishing of the sense of oneness of the meditative experience. When these signs manifest, the mind is about to go off and follow some distraction. If the distraction can be caught at that moment (or a bit afterward), the mind's evident wish for something more active can be accommodated by way of shifting to the respective insight reflection, regarding what has been left behind with the perception of infinite space. In this way, practice goes along with the natural vagaries of the mind but in a way that keeps it within the trajectory of the gradual meditation on emptiness. Once the reflection has fulfilled its purpose, the mind will often tend to become quieter and thereby ready to return to silent abiding. In this way, skillfully weaving a continuity of practice by alternating between periods of silent abiding and moments of reflective insight can be a very enjoyable and flexible approach that at the same time is highly effective.

By way of conclusion to my exploration of practice-related aspects of the present step, below I translate a poem that hopefully captures some of the points covered above. In my translation, I leave out a part that broaches a topic not relevant to my present concerns. The first part of the poem describes the nature of space as trackless. The remainder of the poem then takes up the tendency of common people to delight in conceptual proliferation, a negative term representative of going along with the unending stream of thoughts and associations that often completely overwhelm the untrained mind. In contrast to such common people, those who have reached full awakening are free from conceptual proliferation. In other words, fully awakened ones—here referred to with the term "thus gone ones"—are free from conceptual proliferation, just as space is free from tracks:[90]

> Indeed, there is no track in empty space ...
> Common people delight in conceptual proliferation;
> Thus gone ones are free from conceptual proliferation.

5. Summary

Although the perception of infinite space corresponds to the object taken by the first of the four immaterial spheres, in the present context its meditative use does not require a comparable depth of concentration. In line with the overall trajectory of a meditative conjunction of tranquility and insight, the emphasis can be on cultivating mindfulness of the notion of infinite space, in order to be able to shift easily between calm abiding and an understanding of the disturbances that have been left behind.

A powerful way of establishing equanimity in regard to whatever may occur at any of the six senses is to keep the mind like space. As an ingenious middle path between suppression and avoidance, the mind that is open and receptive like space still takes in all the information needed but avoids compulsive reactivity to it. Cultivated in this way, equanimity can be established at each sense door in a swift manner, illustrated with the following series of similes:

seeing:	closing or opening the eyes
hearing:	snapping a finger
smelling:	a raindrop rolling off a sloping lotus leaf
tasting:	bending or extending an arm
touching:	spitting out a ball of spittle
thinking:	water drops evaporating on a heated iron plate

Cultivating a space-like mind can help to maintain a nonreactive attitude toward various challenges, whose lack of effect on the mind can be similar to someone attempting to paint on space. Relating the same imagery to the five hindrances, maintaining a space-like mind in the face of a hindrance that emerges during meditation can render the hindrance powerless. It becomes unable to color the space of the mind with sensuality, make it boil in anger, cover it with the algae of sloth-and-torpor, agitate it through the wind of restlessness-and-worry, or shroud it in darkness through doubt.

Another helpful notion can be found in the quality of being unestablished. This term qualifies not only Nirvana and the consciousness of awakened ones but also space. Finding inspiration in such connotations can provide a boost to the present practice, by way of attempting to resemble, to whatever degree this is possible within the limits of our personal situation, the mental attitude of awakened ones, through staying free from defilements and unwholesome reactivity. The resultant inner freedom compares to the trackless nature of empty space.

6. Practical Instructions

Actual practice begins by proceeding through the steps mentioned in the previous chapters: setting our motivation, physical seclusion, mental seclusion, perception of earth, and then the other three elements up to a body scan related to the wind element. Once this has been completed, another body scan can be done in the understanding that the manifestation of the wind element requires space. The scan can begin by becoming aware of the space occupied by the head and from there move to the neck, shoulders, arms, hands, torso, pelvis, legs, and feet, each time aware of the space occupied by these parts of the body. This then naturally leads to becoming aware of the whole body from the viewpoint of the space it occupies. In this way, comparable to some extent to the idea in ancient Indian cosmology that the Earth ultimately rests on space, similarly the earth in the human body relies on the space occupied by the body. By paying attention to the whole body from the viewpoint of space, it becomes possible to allow our own body to dissolve into space, to become space, as it were.

Resting in awareness of the whole body that has dissolved into space can then be combined with the recognition that space by its nature is without boundaries. This can help in letting go of the subjective sense of a boundary between the space occupied by the body and the space that surrounds it on all sides, leading to a perception of space as present in all directions.

In order to interrelate the inner experience of space and its outer counterpart, the same procedure done earlier for the earth element can be employed, in the sense of becoming aware of the ground below, but now from the viewpoint of its space rather than its solidity, and then zooming out again to cover the whole region, state, continent, the whole planet, and eventually going beyond even that to arrive at an awareness of the whole universe. This can result in the subjective experience of becoming one with the whole universe. Infinite space is without limit, without center; it is unobstructed, and it has no ups and no downs and none of the four directions.

Allowing the whole body to dissolve into space can at times cause fear or be unsettling, simply because it is a way of relating to our own embodied experience that is rather unusual. Such reactivity is only natural. A sense of reassurance can be established by first of all softly backing up to whole-body awareness as a way of grounding, and then establishing an attitude of *mettā/maitrī* to relax the mind and prevent it from contracting or closing down. At a later time, when things have calmed down, it can be helpful to reflect that the body and all things are indeed for the most part made up of space. Hence, cultivating the perception of the spatial nature of material phenomena is a way of counterbalancing a lopsided view of how we normally view these phenomena. These are neither just matter nor just space. But since we are so accustomed to look at them as just matter, some training in seeing the other and complementary dimension of space can help to have a more accurate apperception of reality.

The idea is obviously not to pretend that everything is only space and we can now cross a street without needing to look out for traffic. This form of practice is not meant to encourage a form of spacing out. The four elements do exist as qualities, and the preceding practice has clarified that on an experiential level. But there is more to reality than just that, and with the present perception a dimension of material phenomena can be acknowledged that so far has probably not received the attention it deserves. No wonder that taking this dimension into account can be experienced as unsettling. In fact, the more unsettling it appears, the more lopsided has been our way of seeing material phenomena so far. Clarifying this is not meant to encourage a forceful approach. To the contrary, whenever reactivity manifests, it is of crucial importance to take things slowly and gently, with *mettā/maitrī* allowing us to ease into the new perspective that is opening up. Reactivity is natural and, from an overall perspective of inner growth, even a positive sign, as it shows that ingrained ways of seeing things are being put into question.

Another point is also to check for possible associations of space with loneliness and coldness. As mentioned above, there are several ways that can help arouse positive connotations of space, by way of noting its creative potential or else by way of relating it to the divine abodes. The very presence of space provides the potentiality for everything to happen. Even these words would not be legible without the space provided by the blank paper that serves as their background; without the space between the book or digital file and the eyes of the reader, it would not be possible to read them. Reflecting in this and other related ways can help to arouse positive associations with the notion of space. Space is by definition complete. It never lacks anything and is always there. What more could there be to look for?

Actually, as with the perception of earth, proper cultivation of the perception of space increases connectedness to others rather than decreasing it. What it decreases is the solidified sense of being a separate self. But for that to decrease is actually quite welcome. Perception of space can indeed to a considerable degree soften the edges of the dualistic contrast between myself and others. Moreover, the infinite space of the whole universe is not just a blank nothing. From the viewpoint of early Buddhist cosmology, it is pervaded by the presence of all those deceased meditators of the past who achieved the attainment of the sphere of infinite space. These are now reborn in this condition and will continue living for incredibly long periods of time in it. By attending to the perception of the sphere of infinite space, we enter at least to some degree in communion with those who have achieved the full attainment and those meditators of the past who have been reborn and now abide in this condition.

Another problem that can manifest in the beginning stages of practice is that the idea of infinite space seems merely conceptual and does not really sink in. This is only natural and requires simply allowing the practice to mature gradually. In addition, it may be helpful to bring in a bit of meditative activity. Throughout, mindfulness monitors and thereby provides the information needed to decide if and to what degree becoming active is appropriate in the present moment, given the actual condition of the mind. An active implementation could take the form of mentally reaching out into the forward direction, allowing attention to keep traveling forward in the understanding that it is passing through space. Material objects are not an obstruction, as these can be viewed from the perspective of the space they occupy, thereby allowing them to become part of the perception of space. However far attention reaches out in front, it will not be able to reach an ending point. The space in front is indeed infinite. With the infinity of space established in this way, attention can move similarly to the right, back, and left, thereby extending the same infinitude of space to all four directions. This can be visualized as a broadening or extension of the awareness already established in front. In other words, there is no need to relinquish awareness of infinite space in front in order to establish it to the right, etc. The next step would then be to do the same upward and then downward into the ground, viewed from the perspective of the space it occupies, thereby allowing that to dissolve into space as well. In this way, a perception of infinite space in all directions can be gradually established and thereby come to appear less abstract and a bit more something that is actually experienced.

Needless to say, the above is just meant as one possible way to approach the cultivation of the perception of infinite space, and practitioners should feel free to adjust to personal preferences. Throughout, it can be helpful to remind ourselves that space is already there; it is not something that has to be created or made. There is no need to strive or strain, and if there is even a trace of getting tense, the appropriate response to that is just relaxing and allowing the perception of space to arise out of that very condition of relaxation and letting go of tension. In the end, what counts is finding some way that works for becoming effortlessly aware of infinite space in a way that also facilitates mental composure and helps avoid distractions. The final aim is invariably just abiding in the perception of infinite space without any further activity. That is, if some reaching out in the different directions, etc., has been employed, it should be clear that this is just a crutch for gradually progressing to a stage where the crutch is no longer needed.

If at any time distractions arise during the initial arousal or subsequent abiding in infinite space, a smiling recognition of the ingrained tendency of the mind to run after what is not really worth being pursued can become the starting point for recovering the present moment by way of introducing some degree of spaciousness in the mind. This can be visualized as surrounding the thought or daydream with space and thereby depriving it of any solid ground on which to stand. Thoughts or daydreams require to some extent a narrow mental condition in order to thrive. Lacking that, at times they just dissolve into space on their own. By its very nature, space is not established anywhere. Attending to the perception of infinite space, at least to some extent the mind comes to share this unestablished nature. This leaves no landing place for defilements to establish themselves and to color the mind, heat it up, cover it, stir it around, or shroud it in darkness. By its very nature, space can never become unbalanced. Hence, cultivating a mind like space can lead to becoming firmly established in this condition of being naturally balanced.

In case distractions manifest in a prolonged manner and the strategy of the space-like mind does not seem to work, it can be preferable to move backward through the perception of earth to seclusion, perhaps even taking time to cultivate the divine abodes. Once the mind has settled down, the time has come to proceed again forward step by step, until reaching the perception of infinite space. This serves as a way of giving the mind something to do and thereby makes it easier to achieve a basic degree of mental unification.

Once mental collectedness has been reestablished at least to some degree, awareness of the breath can be a helpful tool for maintaining continuity in the abiding in infinite space whenever the mind tends toward becoming distracted. As earlier, the appropriate approach is peripheral awareness of the breath as something that takes place in the background. With such peripheral awareness of the process of breathing, the perception of infinite space can remain in the foreground of the attentional field. At times, practice can adjust to the rhythm of the breath through slight shifts of attention. With the inbreath, a bit more attention could be given to the quality of space as not established anywhere, to the perception of all materiality having dissolved into space. With the outbreath, a bit more attention could then be given to the infinity of space outside, to its boundless and unlimited nature. When undertaken in this way, the meditative abiding comes with a rhythmic alternation between being more aware of the dissolution of materiality through space and being more aware of the infinite nature of space, of the absence of any limit or ending point. When effortlessly abiding in infinite space, however, such paying of attention to the breath may not be appropriate and might even disturb the calm abiding in the present step in the gradual meditation on emptiness. Hence, the suggestion to rely on the breath is only meant as a tool in case the mind tends to get distracted. By way of concluding the session of formal meditation, whenever this seems opportune, from infinite space a brief return to the perceptions of earth and of the forest can complete the meditative trajectory, followed by dedicating our merit.

Beyond formal meditation practice, the perception of space can continue to impact daily life. Walking meditation can become walking through space. In fact, anything done at the physical level can be combined with an awareness of ourselves being surrounded by space. This can involve the same practice of embodied mindfulness as earlier, with the difference that the body is experienced from the viewpoint of it being surrounded by space. Attention in a way zooms out a little bit and takes into account the immediate environment in which the body is positioned.

Having learned to note space in this or other ways will in turn make it easier to apply the same perception during challenging situations. An example would be becoming aware of the space between us and others, which can be a remarkably powerful tool for facing difficult communications and relational problems. Giving others the space they need and becoming more spacious around difficult issues will substantially impact social interactions. Even just noticing the silence between words as a manifestation of space, or the gap between one breath and another, can serve as a reminder of space. Throughout, space can be introduced into any situation and thereby serve as a reminder of the ultimately empty nature of all phenomena.

V. Infinite Consciousness

Again, Ānanda, not attending to the perception of earth and not attending to the perception of the sphere of infinite space, a monastic attends to oneness in dependence on the perception of the sphere of infinite consciousness. Their mind enters upon, is pleased with, settles on, and is devoted to the perception of the sphere of infinite consciousness.

They understand like this: "Whatever disturbances there could be in dependence on the perception of earth, these are not present here. Whatever disturbances there could be in dependence on the perception of the sphere of infinite space, these are not present here. There is just this remainder of disturbance, namely the oneness in dependence on the perception of the sphere of infinite consciousness."

They understand: "This perceptual range is empty of the perception of earth"; and they understand: "This perceptual range is empty of the perception of the sphere of infinite space. There is just this non-emptiness, namely the oneness in dependence on the perception of the sphere of infinite consciousness."

Thus, they contemplate it as empty of what is indeed not there, and they understand that what remains there is still present: "It is there." Ānanda, like this there also comes to be for them this genuine, undistorted, and purified entry into emptiness.[91]

1. The Nature of Consciousness

An appreciation of the above instructions calls for a closer look at the early Buddhist conception of consciousness. The term "consciousness" (Pāli: *viññāṇa*; Sanskrit: *vijñāna*) is one of several alternative terms employed in early Buddhist texts to refer to the mind. Another such term is *citta*, which often refers to the heart-mind, in the sense of the mind as the seat of emotions and as that which is amenable to transformation through meditative training. Yet another such term is *manas*, whose import could perhaps be captured as the intellect-mind. *Manas* serves as the sixth sense in addition to the five physical senses and as the agent of mental activity when differentiated from physical and verbal activity. Compared to these two, consciousness does not carry such active nuances, standing predominantly for a receptive type of knowing that results from contact between a sense and its object. In terms of meditation-related tasks, whereas the "heart-mind" (*citta*) should be cultivated and the "intellect-mind" (*manas*) should be restrained, consciousness should be comprehended with insight. Although it is thus possible to point out distinct nuances of meaning for these three terms, such distinctions are not set in stone; in fact, at times these three terms occur together as three near synonyms.[92]

At times, consciousness on its own represents the whole of the mind. An instance of such usage occurs in a description of the attitude of an arahant/arhat, who is completely free from any self-notion or appropriation in regard to earth, water, fire, wind, space, and consciousness.[93] The listing of the four elements, space, and consciousness is meant to comprise all aspects of experience, as the purpose is to showcase the complete absence of self-notions or appropriations in an arahant. Due to an emphasis on the material dimension, this particular type of description analyzes matter in detail but refers to the mental side of experience simply with the generic term "consciousness."

As the fifth of the five aggregates, however, consciousness stands only for one aspect of the mind, distinct from the other three mental aggregates of feeling tones, perceptions, and volitional activities. Perception, for example, refers to the part of the mind that recognizes and differentiates, whereas consciousness is a receptive knowing of whatever happens in subjective experience. This distinction gets to some extent blurred in two Pāli passages that define consciousness in a way that would better suit perception. Comparative study shows that in both cases the parallels offer a more compelling definition that considers the role of consciousness to be that which knows experiences arisen in dependence on one of the six senses and the respective objects.[94] This concords better with the way the early discourses usually depict consciousness.

The presentation by way of the six senses does not posit consciousness as some sort of unitary entity that avails itself of various possible avenues of experience. Instead, the idea is rather that there are six types of consciousness, which are distinct from each other. There is eye-consciousness, for example, whose function concerns the sense door of the eye and not any other sense door. The key point behind such a way of presentation is to make it unmistakably clear that consciousness is a dependently arisen phenomenon; it is not some sort of permanent entity. The early discourses quite explicitly state that it is impossible to find any consciousness that is permanent.[95] In short, consciousness is not an entity but a process.

Seeing that even consciousness is subject to the law of impermanence is challenging. Due to its nature of just receptively knowing, consciousness does not seem to exhibit change in a manner comparable to the other mental aggregates. Feeling tones change from pleasant to painful or neutral, perceptions quite obviously differ from each other, and volitional reactions to what is experienced are also not the same. In contrast, the bare receptive knowing part of subjective experience seems to stay the same with all such experiences. Hence, such knowing of what is taking place can more easily be mistaken to be permanent.

Nevertheless, thorough inspection can show such a conclusion to be unconvincing. If the knowing of what happens were permanent, it would forever be frozen in the condition of knowing just one thing. The very fact that consciousness can be conscious of different things implies that the act of knowing must also be of a changing nature. Consciousness is nothing but such acts of knowing; it is not an entity that is distinct from the activity of knowing.

The nature of consciousness as a potential source of delusion comes to the fore in a series of similes that illustrate the empty nature of each of the five aggregates of clinging. In this setting, consciousness compares to a magical illusion.[96] The simile describes a magician displaying such a magical illusion at a crossroads. In the ancient setting, such crossroads were apparently the type of place where one would put up a show or try to sell something. A passerby with keen eyes sees through the magical illusion and finds it to be thoroughly empty. In the same way, we should see through consciousness in order to discern its thoroughly empty nature.

2. Name-and-Form

An exploration of the empty nature of consciousness can be related to a particularly intriguing perspective on its conditioned nature, which emerges in the context of descriptions of dependent arising (Pāli: *paṭicca samuppāda*; Sanskrit: *pratītya samutpāda*). This takes the form of a reciprocal conditioning relationship between consciousness and name-and-form.[97] Here, "name" stands for those mental factors responsible for the arousal of a concept, for quite literally giving something its "name"—feeling tone, perception, intention, contact, and attention—whereas "form" represents the material side of experience.[98] Name and form together provide the *content* of experience, its *appearance*, whereas consciousness can be seen as the *presence* of experience.[99] Presence and content depend on each other.[100] Without the presence of knowing, there is no known content; without known content, there is no presence of knowing. In the same way, consciousness is the condition for name-and-form, just as name-and-form is the condition for consciousness.

Instead of speaking of the presence and content of experience, an alternative way of attempting to convey the gist of the same matter would be to consider consciousness as representing *actuality* whereas name-and-form stands for *potentiality*.[101] That is, the presence of consciousness ensures that experience *actually* takes place. However, what that experience will be, its *potential*, is in the hands of name-and-form. Name determines what will be attended to, in what way this will be felt and perceived, and, perhaps most importantly, how we will react to it.

The function of each of the five aspects of name in processing experience could be illustrated by relating these five aspects to the five fingers of a hand:[102] feeling tone can be taken to correspond to the little finger, perception to the ring finger, volition to the middle finger, contact to the index finger, and attention to the thumb. Although this simile is not found in the early discourses, the count of "five" (*pañca*), whose role in ancient Indian discourse as representative of a complete unit appears to go back to the five fingers of a hand, is etymologically closely related to "conceptual proliferation" (Pāli: *pa-pañca*; Sanskrit: *pra-pañca*).[103] In view of this etymological relationship, it does not seem too farfetched to propose that conceptual proliferation occurs when the five fingers of name get quite literally out of hand.

Such getting out of hand anyway needs to be avoided, which holds all the more for the present stage of emptiness meditation. The challenge is to step out of involvement with conceptual proliferation and elaboration and to learn to be instead just with the receptive and uninvolved knowing. As a way of hopefully providing some aid for such purposes, an illustration of the five "fingers" of name can make it easier to recognize and counter their sometimes quite mischievous activity.

The little finger, representing feeling tone, is easily overlooked, even though no hand is complete without the little finger. The influence of feeling tone on determining our attitudes and reactions is as easily overlooked as the little finger. Yet, it is fundamental. Feeling tone is prominent at the first moment of contact, and its hedonic quality tends to impact and reverberate through whatever happens subsequently in the mind. Much of apparently reasonable thought can turn out to be just a rationalization of the initial input provided by feeling tone in terms of stimulating likes and dislikes, or else lack of interest.

This can be related to the role of the little finger as the one we would choose to wear a signet ring. Feeling tone functions comparably to a signet, as it seals the deal of experience through its hedonic quality: pleasant feeling tone as positive and painful feeling tone as negative, which is being stamped on experience, with the alternative option of neutral feeling tone leading to a dismissal as uninteresting or boring.

The ring finger receives its name from its traditional association in Western societies with wedding rings. The role of perception can indeed be related to marriage. This type of marriage, however, is not necessarily based on a conscious decision to become engaged. Much rather, it is part of a construction of experience that usually goes unnoticed. In the world of experience, perception functions by "marrying" the information that has become available through the senses with whatever seems relevant in the mind's store of memories and associations.

Such a marriage performs an important role in making sense of experience, and even fully awakened ones will still have perception operating. In the case of all those who are not yet fully awakened, however, the operation of perception only too easily brings in prejudices and biases, experienced as aspects of outer reality rather than as what they really are: subjective projections. In this way, perception is indeed the place of marriage between the subjective and the apparently objective.

The middle finger is the longest of the five fingers of a hand. It has a central function in finger snapping, together with the thumb. The length of the middle finger can be related to volition, which is the mental factor that indeed sticks out and has the most long-ranging repercussions, in particular in the form of karma. In the ancient Indian setting, an emphasis on the central role of volition in relation to performing karma appears to have been a distinct position taken by early Buddhism.

The basic principle here is that the intention behind a particular deed can determine if a breach of ethical conduct has taken place. For example, if something was taken out of a wish to steal, the perpetrator has committed a breach of the rule against theft. Without such an intention, however, the same act does not have such repercussions. All of this converges on the central importance of the middle finger of volition. In conjunction with the thumb of attention it can act like a finger snap, by way of calling attention to what appears to be particularly relevant from the viewpoint of our intentions and motivation.

The index finger, or forefinger, serves to point things out. This gesture tends to be done by babies as young as one year old. Thus, the index finger is involved in a very early form of communication in the development of a human being. In a comparable way, contact serves to point things out. Just as when we want to do any work, a place for doing it needs to be found, so contact is the place for experience to occur, where the conjunction of sense organ and sense object can take place, together with the respective type of consciousness. In other words, contact provides the site for experience.

The index finger is also quite dexterous compared to the other fingers already mentioned. At the construction site of contact, a similar adroitness can be witnessed, which involves a constructor and the construction material. These are respectively the other factors of name (the constructor) and the presence of form (the construction material). In the case of formless meditative attainments (such as infinite space and infinite consciousness, etc.), the constructor has in a way run out of material supplies but keeps constructing nonetheless.

With the experience of Nirvana, even the constructor will be left behind. Since the construction site only exists as long as some construction is being done, at this point the site will also be abandoned. When cessation is "contacted," contact ceases. This in turn serves as the ultimate confirmation of the insubstantial nature of experience and the fact that even contact, as the site for mental construction, is itself constructed.

The thumb is the finger that clinches a deal. We will put up the thumb to signify approval, just as by putting it down we can convey the opposite. The thumb is the finger most needed to take hold of things. The role of attention is indeed to take hold of things, by way of determining which aspect of experience will now be attended to. In this function, attention can also be considered as particularly versatile among the factors of name, just as the thumb is the most flexible of all five fingers in terms of movement.

By singling out what is of interest, attention functions to some extent comparably to an evaluation, by way of giving a thumbs-up or thumbs-down. In the minds of those who have not yet reached full awakening, such evaluations often involve attention that is unwise or superficial (*ayoniso*) rather than being wise or penetrative (*yoniso*). Whereas the former leads to bondage, the latter leads to liberation. Hence, the crucial question with attention is how it is being deployed.

Both types of deployment of attention involve the other fingers of the hand. All five fingers are required for a fully functional hand. In the same way, all of the five factors of name are required for fully functional mental operations. They indeed remain operative even in an arahant. The crucial difference is only that the five fingers of an arahant no longer get out of hand: they no longer produce conceptual proliferation.

3. Subduing Name-and-Form

The task with the present stage in the gradual meditation on emptiness can be understood as a subduing of name-and-form so that consciousness comes to be the dominant feature of subjective experience. As far as form is concerned, this much has already been accomplished previously, as with the perception of infinite space all experiences related to materiality have been left behind.

The subduing of name can in turn take as its starting point the role of the "thumb" of attention. Usually, attention is very much involved with the other factors of name, as if the thumb has been deeply buried in the fist. The situation need not be like this, however, as it is also possible to take the thumb out and stretch it in the opposite direction, similar to what we would do in order to communicate thumbs-up or thumbs-down. Taking out the thumb of attention in this way can illustrate directing attention to the type of consciousness that arises at any sense door, rather than to the sense object.

In principle, any sense experience involves a particular object, such as, in the present case of reading, the visible object of written words, the corresponding sense, which right now is the sense door of the eyes, and the corresponding type of consciousness, which is eye-consciousness. Even now, while reading, it is possible to continue reading but become more aware of the act of seeing through the eyes than of the paper or digital file that is being read. Taking a further step, it is even possible to continue reading and at the same time be aware of the part of the mind that knows the experience of reading. This is consciousness, that is, eye-consciousness in this particular example. Maybe try once again? Attention can proceed from its natural object in the form of the page in front of the eyes to shining the light of awareness also on the act of seeing through the eyes and then even on the presence in the mind of an act of knowing that something is being seen.

The same turning inward toward that which knows can be achieved with sound. The normal tendency on hearing a sound is to turn toward its source and try to identify what it is. The five fingers are fully active. Instead of following the ingrained rut of how we usually perceive the world, however, it is possible to opt for pointing the thumb of attention toward the ear sense door. This diminishes the tendency of the mind to become involved with the five fingers of name and then get lost in conceptual proliferation and reactivity of various types toward what has just been heard. Due to attention being at the ear sense door, there is less of a tendency to locate the sound outside and then comment on it, instead of which there can be more emphasis on the act of hearing.

Taking this still a step further could then involve pointing the thumb of attention away from the other fingers and toward the stillness of that which knows, of consciousness. The progression would thus be from something being heard, via hearing, to the knowing of the sound. With each step in this progression, the activity of name becomes more subdued, and there is less of a tendency to proliferate the heard in various ways.

The effect of sustained practice undertaken in this way could be illustrated by borrowing a simile used in the Pāli discourses to illustrate the second absorption, a condition of deep mental tranquility. The illustration of this mental condition describes a lake fed solely by a spring of water from within, not being replenished by any inflow of water coming from the four directions outside or even by rain.[104] The import of this image is to convey the thorough pervasion of the meditator with nonsensual joy and happiness experienced during the attainment of the second absorption.

Applied to the present context, the image of this lake could be used in a different way, namely as an illustration of the nature of consciousness in its role of just knowing what occurs at a sense door, as distinct from the activity of name in processing what occurs by making sense of it and reacting to it. This role of consciousness could be compared to the lake, which reflects whatever occurs on the outside. At times the sun shines, at other times there may be clouds, or else on a moonless night the whole environment could become pitch dark. Even though the lake reflects the brightness of the sunlight, the grayish color of the clouds, and the darkness of the night, this is just a reflection; the clarity of the water of the lake itself remains the same throughout. In the same way, consciousness just reflects what occurs at a sense door, together with what name makes out of it, without consciousness itself necessarily being affected by it. Directing attention to consciousness rather than being fully involved with name compares to attending to the natural clarity of the lake rather than to its bright, gray, or dark appearance due to the influence of outer circumstances.

At the same time, however, it needs to be noted that the lake is not an entity but a constantly changing phenomenon. Even though the lake appears to be still, water keeps moving into it from the spring within and keeps evaporating on its surface. That is, behind its appearance as a stable body of water stands a subtle motion not readily perceptible to the eyes. Consciousness is similar, and any reification of it needs to be avoided in the understanding that it is definitely impermanent, being just a process of knowing, a consciousness-ing, so to say. With this proviso in place, learning to give pride of place to consciousness rather than its objects can go a long way in introducing an inner reference point of stillness and stability that enables handling the ups and downs of life so much better. It not only facilitates introducing the crucial brief pause of fully apperceiving the available information before reacting, as it also provides a grounding in calmness that helps counter agitation. In fact, even if there is agitation, stirred up by name in one way or another, just turning to that which is aware of the agitation can open a door to the still lake within that is not affected by whatever it reflects. In this way, turning to that which knows can help reveal the construction of experience and the central role of our own mental activities in influencing, shaping, and modeling the things that are experienced as being out there.

A Pāli verse eloquently expresses the primacy of the mind in a way that can be taken as an inspiration for such practice. The context is a teaching on karma and its fruit, in relation to which our own mind is of course the key factor. The first part of the verse in question proceeds as follows:[105]

> Phenomena are preceded by the mind,
> They are led by the mind,
> And they are made by the mind.

4. Summary

"Consciousness" is one of several terms used in early Buddhism to refer to the mind. It is not an entity, but much rather a conditioned and impermanent process of knowing, whose arising depends on contact between a sense door and its corresponding object.

The continuity of experience rests on the reciprocal conditioning between consciousness on the one side and name-and-form on the other. The activity of name can be illustrated with the five fingers of a hand. The little finger, the one usually used to wear a signet ring, compares to the input provided by the three feeling tones (pleasant, painful, neutral): it seals the deal of experience and stamps it with approval, rejection, or disinterest. The ring finger of perception marries sense data with personal biases and associations, pretending that the resultant evaluations are inherent in the sense objects, rather than originating in our own mind. The middle finger of volition sticks out among all else, as the way we react to what is perceived shapes our own future. The index finger of contact points to the event of experience taking place. The thumb of attention decides which aspect of a particular moment will be attended to.

Although usually the thumb of attention is busily occupied with the other fingers of name, comparable to being buried in a clenched fist, it can in principle be used differently. It can point to the sense door instead of the sense object, or even to the respective consciousness. The last option can become a powerful tool for daily-life practice as well as for revealing the primacy of our own mind in the construction of experience.

5. Practical Instructions

Practice of the present step builds on the steps mentioned in the previous chapters. After we have set our motivation, awareness can turn to physical seclusion and its complement in mental seclusion, then to the perception of earth, followed by proceeding through the other three elements up to space. Shifting from the space occupied by the body to infinite space can come to include the whole universe.

The next step in the gradual meditation on emptiness involves a shift from space to consciousness as that which knows space. Due to having taken infinite space as its object, consciousness has itself become infinite. Increasing familiarity with the overall progression of the practice will allow executing the shift from one perception to the next fairly swiftly. However, when first getting started with this type of practice, in order to develop a distinct sense of the underlying dynamics, it would be commendable to deepen and mature the experience of infinite space for some time until it has become established sufficiently well, both in the sense of meditative familiarity and in the sense of appreciating its insight-related implications, before proceeding to infinite consciousness.

The perceptual shift to be executed at the present juncture requires turning from the object to the subject, in the sense of becoming aware of that which knows. Out of the three aspects of experience at any sense door—the object, the sense faculty, and the corresponding type of consciousness—the latter usually goes unnoticed and is somewhat taken for granted. In a way this is only natural, as the exciting things appear to happen out there, and what takes place in here seems to be considerably less interesting. Yet, sustained training with the present step will reveal that the really fascinating part is much rather what happens in here. Allowing the process of knowing to be more explicitly attended to and acknowledged in this way can benefit from experimenting in various ways during daily-life situations with such a shift of attention, in the sense of a turning inward toward that which knows. Familiarity developed in this way prepares the ground for being able to execute the same shift in formal meditation with more ease.

At times it can be helpful to proceed once more through different spatial directions in the manner employed previously to establish the perception of infinite space, just to have already familiar ground to work with, but done from the perspective of the knowing of space rather than just space as such. In other words, becoming aware of space in front from the viewpoint of it being known, then space to the right, back, left, above, and below, all the time giving importance to the knowing of space in all directions. This is only meant as a crutch and will no longer be relevant with increasing familiarity and in the absence of distractions, when a direct shift from infinite space to infinite consciousness will often be the most appropriate way of proceeding.

Whenever distractions arise, the same shift to that which knows can suffice to ensure continuity of the practice. This takes things a step further compared to the previously adopted strategy of surrounding the distracting thought or daydream with space. The present procedure handles distraction by directing attention to the knowing part of the mind, which by dint of its receptive nature is not involved in the agitation created by the fingers of mental activity. Experimenting with this tool can further confirm the vital discovery that meditation does not require the absence of thought. What it does require, however, is the presence of mindfulness to enable the recognition that there is thought activity. But there is no need to use force to stop that thought activity. Instead, a gentle and relaxed turning to that which knows can provide a haven in the storm, an anchoring in stillness that can never be really perturbed, no matter what type of frolic and gambol there might be.

Should the frolic and gambol be of such intensity that we are unable to stay with the inner anchor in stillness, mindfulness recognizes that the time has come to back up, returning to a more structured approach based on going backward through the previous practices that have been used to build up to the present perception. After that has been completed, the time has come to move forward again. With growing familiarity, however, such backing up will become less and less necessary, as it becomes increasingly easy to take the thumb of attention out of its close association with the other four fingers of name and point it instead at the knowing part of the mind. This knowing part is always available, as it is part of any moment of experience. Although with some experiences this is more challenging and with others easier, the possibility of turning to stillness within is always in principle available, anytime and anywhere. In fact, with growing familiarity and expertise, the more challenging situations will become the most interesting opportunities for exploring the potential of turning to that which knows. It is right at the time when things go "wrong" and we are about to become reactive and upset that the present perception can be of major help.

Continuity of our abiding in the perception of infinite consciousness during formal meditation can be strengthened by relying on the same peripheral awareness of the breath already cultivated earlier in relation to other perceptions. In the present case, the difference is that the inbreath can come with an awareness of the mind as the source and platform of all experiences, a recognition that, in a way, there is only the mind. The exhalation in turn can serve as a reminder of the infinite nature of consciousness, which by its nature has no boundaries or limits (unless these are imposed on it).

Increasing familiarity with this step in the gradual meditation on emptiness can lead to experiencing anything that happens as taking place *within* our own mind. This is not to take an idealist position and deny that things exist even when we do not cognize them. That would be taking things too far. But for anything to exist for us subjectively, we need to cognize it. Hence, in a way, the whole world known to us is comprised within our own mind. Therefore, whatever takes place is indeed happening within our own mind. Hearing a sound can come with the realization that it is resonating in our own mind. Visions, odors, tastes, and tangibles, which to all appearances have their source somewhere outside, can all be viewed as occurring within the mind itself.

Practice done in this way can offer a remarkably transformative approach for going through life. Compared to ordinary modes of functioning, this approach is similar to the difference between watching a movie while being totally carried away by what happens on the screen and watching it while remaining aware that it is just a movie after all. The drama of existence is to a considerable degree a fabrication of our own mind, which provides the stage and then, based on the script it composed, acts out this drama, even though we usually do not openly admit that and prefer to pretend to be an innocent spectator.

The understanding that grows in this way relates to the disturbance or weariness left behind at this stage, which is the taking up of objects. The key aspect here is a stepping out of the subject-object duality, the basic bifurcation of experience that is so deeply ingrained in the way we relate to the world. Turning attention to infinite consciousness, to the unlimited nature of that which knows, implies that any other object has been left behind. This could be conceived as a dropping of all objects altogether or alternatively as turning the subject into its own object. Whichever way of viewing this matter may be more appealing, the key is a shift toward mind only. Again, just to make sure this point is not missed, this is just a soteriological tool and not an ontological truth claim. It is just an approach to become more aware of the degree to which subjectivity impacts what happens and to counter the ingrained tendency to overlook what we contribute ourselves to the problems and challenges we encounter.

The present step leaves behind the disturbance and weariness of the usual fragmentation of experience, achieved by relinquishing all objects apart from the mind as such. It carries considerable potential in bringing about mental composure and unification of the mind.[106] The basic pattern is simply attending to that dimension of the mind where all the various experiences converge, which is that which knows or consciousness. This mode of attending can provide composure during any activity and can also be used as a launching pad for the formal cultivation of deeper levels of mental unification during sitting meditation.

At the same time, however, such leaving behind of the usual fragmentation of experience goes beyond the experience of mental unification possible through deeper levels of mental composure, as it addresses the very root of the bifurcation of experience. Due to this more thorough cutting through, it has a strong transformative potential that can pervade every aspect of daily life. It can result in the presence of an imperturbable element of clarity and often also manifest in a subtle type of wholesome joy due to remaining established in the present moment by way of awareness of the knowing aspect of experience.

The preceding perception of infinite space offers an avenue for appreciating the nature of matter as consisting for the most part just of space. The perception of infinite consciousness can in turn lead to a better appreciation of the fact that the subject cannot be completely separated from the object, pretending that they are so fundamentally different that the former has no impact on the latter. The present step in the gradual meditation on emptiness makes the influence of the mind on whatever is observed a matter of direct experience.

Becoming aware of the mind puts the meditator in direct contact with the one thing that can indeed be changed and improved, the one thing that is right at the heart of all the ups and downs in life. Nothing could matter more; nothing could be more promising. In fact, just turning toward that which knows already provides an element of stability that is not directly affected by the vicissitudes of any situation. These tend to impact the name part of the mind much more than consciousness as such.

There is an element of naturalness in turning to that which knows, the recognition of which can help us beware of the pitfalls of either trying to strain forward or else giving up in frustration. The process of practice undertaken here is indeed a natural unfolding, like the blossoming of a beautiful flower. The buds first need time to grow; they will not blossom right away. Space and consciousness are already there; there is no need to construct or fabricate them. The habit patterns of relating to things in ways contrary to their empty nature are deeply ingrained, even though on closer inspection they turn out to be unrealistic and detrimental. There is a need to allow time to change these habit patterns gradually. They cannot be stopped overnight simply by dint of force. Because they are built through repetitions, they can only be undone through repetition, that is, through repeated abiding in emptiness.

At times, some element of inquiry undertaken outside of formal meditation can help to clarify the situation and further deconstruct habitual ways of misperceiving things. Where exactly does the inner dimension end and the outer dimension start? What marks off the apparently quite substantial difference between the subject and the object? Are these not much rather relative notions, dependent on each other and part of a continuum? A simple exercise to play with this type of inquiry could be to close the eyes and sense our embodied presence, followed by opening the eyes and looking at some part of the body, such as the hands, noticing how these change their status from having been part of the felt sense of the subject to becoming the object, in this case the object of vision.

The limits usually imposed on experience begin to dissolve; the artificial boundaries often created out of habit begin to crumble. All converge on the central role of one thing: the mind. The creator of the world of experience is to be found within. The vital impact of motivation becomes unmistakably clear. This is precisely why meditation is of paramount importance: changing the mind is the key to changing the world. This is not to encourage ignoring social injustice but much rather to encourage addressing it from the vantage point of a firm grounding in mental training.

Alongside these benefits, it needs to be noted that there is a danger that the meditative perception of infinite consciousness—and also of other steps in this emptiness practice, such as infinite space—can be turned into an object of attachment. This would be the exact opposite of what they are meant for. The instructions in fact incorporate a hint at the need not to latch on to any of these experiences, by way of drawing attention to the disturbance or weariness that is still present with each of these perceptions. In order to strengthen this rather crucial dimension of the practice, it can be quite helpful to place the meditative trajectory from the outset under the overarching aim of liberation and benefiting others (formulated in some way in our motivation). An altruistic motivation can help us to realize that the path undertaken here is the very opposite of reification or clinging to any of the resultant experiences by appropriating them as "ours" and using them as building blocks for the conceit of being exceptional practitioners. All of this is not about *getting* something but about *shedding* something. It is about letting go, letting go, and again letting go.

By way of conclusion, it will be useful to do the backward tour by turning, at least briefly, to infinite space, earth, and seclusion, perhaps noting how in this way the meditative experience gradually becomes coarser, more on the side of disturbances and weariness. Noticing this can help deepen our appreciation of the nature of each disturbance or weariness when doing the progression again in forward order. The concluding point remains sharing our merits.

Getting ready to move on to whatever is to be done next in daily life, a brief reminder of pointing the thumb of attention toward consciousness can set the proper direction. Whatever happens, whatever we do, there is always the option of doing it while remaining aware of the knowing part of the mind. As a result, any activity can be experienced as happening in the mind. Walking becomes walking within our own mind. Throughout there is a clear recognition of the role of the mind as the stage on which the drama of existence plays out. As a result of such recognition, the dramatizing impact of the play that is right now on stage substantially diminishes.

A gradually growing familiarity with this mode of attending has a remarkable potential to transform our entire life, relationships, and work. It is so simple, in a way, but it takes dedication and time to implement. Instead of turning it into a chore at which we fail and then become frustrated, the best attitude here can be a playful one. Let me see if I can be aware of the knowing mind even once in a whole day? Choosing a particular regular activity as a starting point to build up a habit gradually can be very helpful. Whenever evaluation kicks in with assessments of failure, we just turn around and look at the knowing of such assessments. The very attitude toward the implementation of this practice can benefit considerably from awareness of the knowing mind.

VI. Empty of Self

Again, Ānanda, not attending to the perception of the sphere of infinite space and not attending to the perception of the sphere of infinite consciousness, a monastic attends to oneness in dependence on the perception of the sphere of nothingness. Their mind enters upon, is pleased with, settles on, and is devoted to the perception of the sphere of nothingness.

They understand like this: "Whatever disturbances there could be in dependence on the perception of the sphere of infinite space, these are not present here. Whatever disturbances there could be in dependence on the perception of the sphere of infinite consciousness, these are not present here. There is just this remainder of disturbance, namely the oneness in dependence on the perception of the sphere of nothingness."

They understand: "This perceptual range is empty of the perception of the sphere of infinite space"; and they understand: "This perceptual range is empty of the perception of the sphere of infinite consciousness. There is just this non-emptiness, namely the oneness in dependence on the perception of the sphere of nothingness."

Thus, they contemplate it as empty of what is indeed not there, and they understand that what remains there is still present: "It is there." Ānanda, like this there also comes to be for them this genuine, undistorted, and purified entry into emptiness.[107]

1. Insight and Tranquility

In the course of examining the perception of earth, I noted a basic feature of interrelating tranquility and insight that constitutes an undercurrent of the gradual meditative entry into emptiness (see above p. 48). The pattern of employing perceptions taken from the realm of tranquility—in particular from the immaterial spheres—to cultivate insight into emptiness has a counterpart in another discourse, similarly extant in Pāli, Chinese, and Tibetan, which does the obverse by employing insight contemplations for the cultivation of tranquility. Due to this basic resemblance in meditative cross-fertilization between tranquility and insight, this discourse can conveniently be relied on to develop a practical approach to the present meditative step in the Smaller Discourse on Emptiness.

Although the term "nothingness" can at times refer to the final goal of Buddhist practice,[108] the perception of nothingness employed to cultivate the corresponding immaterial sphere as such does not necessarily involve an insight into emptiness. The Buddha is on record for having gained the actual attainment of the sphere of nothingness during a time in his quest for awakening when he had placed himself under the guidance of an ancient Indian teacher. Even though his teacher was so impressed that he invited him to become a co-teacher, the Buddha-to-be left in the realization that this attainment did not provide the definite answer to the human predicament that he was seeking.[109] This episode illustrates that there is a need to develop a specific modality of the perception of nothingness in order for it to become a tool for insight into emptiness. The discourse presenting insight contemplations as ways to cultivate this tranquility attainment naturally commends itself for this purpose.

The discourse in question presents three alternative approaches for gaining the immaterial sphere of nothingness. One of these relates to a meditative progression for gaining imperturbability, described earlier in the same discourse. Since the Smaller Discourse on Emptiness does not mention such gaining of imperturbability, this approach appears to be less pertinent. Another approach shows quite substantial differences in the three versions, making it uncertain which of these fits the case.[110]

The parallels are in close agreement, however, regarding the remaining approach, whose topic also fits the present context. In the Pāli version, this approach takes the following form: "This is empty of a self and what belongs to a self."[111] The Chinese and Tibetan versions add further details. They specify the Pāli reference to "this" by mentioning the "world," and in addition to the Pāli qualification of being empty of a self and what belongs to a self, they also bring in being empty of permanence and unchangeability.[112] Based on these indications, the contemplation of *nothingness* as a step in the gradual meditation on emptiness can be undertaken in terms of there being *not* a single *thing* in this world of experience that qualifies as a self or as belonging to a self, the latter standing representative of a permanent entity.

Instead of adopting the standard way of rendering as "the sphere of nothingness," an alternative translation of the same Indic term would be "the sphere where nothing is owned."[113] The resultant notion can additionally be relied on as an orientation for the present step of practice, in the sense of calling for a letting go of our sense of ownership (= "belonging to a self") toward whatever is experienced, within or without. This approach can be particularly helpful for actual practice, since a sense of ownership is something we all are well familiar with and can probably identify without much hesitation.

2. Impermanence

The additional reference to the absence of anything permanent in the Chinese and Tibetan versions of the basic contemplation of not self makes explicit what is implicit in the Pāli version, as the early Buddhist conception of not self is intrinsically related to impermanence. Keeping in mind this relationship helps clarify the import of the absence of a self, which is of central relevance within the overall trajectory of contemplating emptiness. Out of the meditative approaches surveyed up to now, being empty of a self goes right to the heart of Buddhist doctrine.

The close relationship between the absence of a self and impermanence emerges repeatedly in the early discourses. A recurrent mode of teaching takes up any part of subjective experience with the inquiry if it is impermanent.[114] Once the listening disciples have acknowledged its impermanence, the follow-up question is whether what is impermanent should be considered as unsatisfactory (*dukkha/duḥkha*). Of course, what changes cannot yield lasting satisfaction; hence what is impermanent is indeed ultimately unsatisfactory. With this much ascertained, the investigation continues with the inquiry if what is impermanent, unsatisfactory, and of a nature to change is fit to be considered a self. In other words, the inappropriateness of considering any aspect of subjective experience as a self is grounded in its impermanent nature.

The same basic pattern can also be seen in a set of insight-related perceptions. This begins with "perception of impermanence." Next comes "perception of unsatisfactoriness in what is impermanent," where what has been ascertained to be impermanent should now be seen as unsatisfactory. Then comes "perception of not self in what is unsatisfactory," where what is unsatisfactory should in turn be recognized as devoid of a self.[115] The internal logic of these three perceptions confirms that the absence of a self is grounded in impermanence via the intermediary of unsatisfactoriness.

A full appreciation of this close reliance of the teaching on the absence of a self on impermanence requires keeping in mind that the above passages stem from a period in the development of Buddhist thought before the arising of the notion of momentariness, according to which everything ceases completely right after having arisen.[116] From an early Buddhist perspective, however, after something has arisen it can continue as a changing process, for a shorter or longer period, before it will cease completely. Whereas the Pāli version of a passage articulating this position just mentions these three phases, a Chinese parallel offers illustrative details. According to its presentation, arising can take the form of being born, ceasing can manifest as passing away, and the interim period of change can then find illustration in loss of teeth, whitening of hair, and an exhaustion of one's physical strength.[117] Such illustrations of aging obviously take time to occur. Although it is in principle possible that someone may pass away right at the time of being born, this is clearly not the norm.

Based on the points that have emerged in this way, the dictum of being empty of a self and what belongs to a self can indeed be understood in terms of being empty of anything permanent, in line with the additional indications given in the Chinese and Tibetan versions of the discourse taken up above. This helps clarify the main import of this aspect of early Buddhist doctrine in a way that directly relates to meditation practice. The contemplation that "this is empty of a self and what belongs to a self," understood as entailing the absence of anything permanent, needs to be applied to consciousness above all else, since this is the one of the five aggregates most easily prone to give rise to the mistaken idea of being some sort of permanent entity.[118] Hence, for the present meditative trajectory to continue from the perception of infinite consciousness to the perception of nothingness makes eminent sense. In this way, the progression of practice ensures that the profound experience of infinite consciousness does not result in mistaken conclusions. In other words, the progression ensures that this experience is, in a way, thoroughly purified of any grasping, however subtle, at a self.

3. Appropriation and Conceit

The problem of the belief in a self as some form of permanent entity will be solved with the realization of stream-entry. With this first breakthrough to the realization of Nirvana,[119] one of the three fetters eradicated on this occasion concerns precisely the view that affirms the existence of such a self.[120] However, this is not yet the complete solution to the problem posed by the notion of a self. Although a stream-enterer no longer subscribes to the idea that such a self exists, ingrained modes of behavior that are based on self-referentiality still need to be overcome. One example is a tendency toward appropriation, or my-making, which calls for adding to the basic assessment that "this is empty of a self" the understanding that it is also empty of "what belongs to a self." Another dimension is conceit, which comes up explicitly in the example quoted above in a recurrent mode of teaching that proceeds from an inquiry regarding impermanence to ascertaining the nature of being unsatisfactory and devoid of a self. The passage in question starts off by indicating that the different modalities of conceit—by way of either feeling superior, feeling (at least) equal, or feeling inferior compared to others—are rooted in not seeing as it really is the impermanent nature of all aspects of subjective experience.[121]

In order to cover these different dimensions of selfing, the standard teaching on not self then calls for contemplating each aspect of subjective reality—usually analyzed by way of the five aggregates of bodily form, feeling tone, perception, volitional activities, and consciousness—in terms of "this is not mine, this I am not, this is not my self."[122] Now, the point of such instruction is not to prohibit words like "I" and "mine." Since appropriation and conceit result from emotional attachment and clinging, the problem cannot be solved just on the linguistic level. In fact, fully awakened ones still use the terms "I" and "mine."[123] In terms of the different modalities of conceit, discussed above, arahants are also able to distinguish between what is superior and what is inferior. An example would be a teaching given reportedly by the Buddha, which distinguishes the appropriateness of serving others based on discerning if through such service one becomes "better" or "worse."[124] The real challenge lies in the presence of emotional attachment and clinging. Hence, the required remedy is to undermine the perceptual underpinning of such attitudes by inculcating a comprehensive awareness of impermanence. The more the fact that everything changes becomes fully ingrained in the mind, penetrating beyond the level of cognitive recognition by transforming its inner attitudes, the more the tendency toward appropriation and conceit will grow weaker, until it can eventually be overcome completely.

The gradual deepening of insight into this crucial dimension of emptiness has a remarkable transformative potential. Putting into question the sense of ownership and control, the notion of some sort of entity that functions as the recipient and administrator of all that is experienced through the senses (including the mind), substantially changes the way we perceive the world. It can introduce a taste of emptiness into the most ordinary activity, simply by letting go of selfing.

This can perhaps be illustrated with the help of a Pāli discourse and its two Chinese parallels, which employ various qualities of the ocean to illustrate dimensions of the Buddha's dispensation. One of these qualities is the taste of the ocean, which is invariably salty. Just as the ocean has the same taste anywhere, so the teachings of the Buddha have the same taste.

According to the Pāli version, this is the taste of liberation.[125] The Chinese parallels mention different but related tastes: one Chinese version speaks of the taste of dispassion, awakening, tranquility, and the path, whereas the other mentions the taste of the noble eightfold path.[126] What these variations have in common is an orientation toward awakening. The same orientation also holds for the specific teaching on emptiness practices explored here, in particular for insight into not self. In terms of the imagery of the ocean pervaded by the same salty taste, with the contemplation of not self all experiences, however they may manifest, can come to be similarly pervaded by the same taste of progress to awakening.

4. Not Self and Conditionality

The crucial aspect of the teaching on the absence of a self as denying the existence of something permanent inherent in a person has not always remained the same in later tradition, where at times an overstatement of this teaching can be found. This shift in perspective can conveniently be illustrated with the simile of a chariot. The original delivery of the chariot simile harks back to a highly realized nun who clarified that a chariot and an individual are composite in nature.[127] Just as a chariot consists of various parts, so an individual consists of the five aggregates.

With later tradition, however, the argument at times becomes that, since a chariot is made up of various parts and therefore can be taken apart, a chariot does not exist at all. The procedure for arriving at this conclusion is to take the chariot apart and then point to its various pieces with the question of whether any of these is the chariot.[128] Of course, none of the parts is the chariot. Yet, it does not follow that there was no chariot before it was taken apart. The term "chariot" refers to a functional assembly of parts with which it is possible to drive. By taking the chariot apart into various pieces, this functional assembly has been destroyed. No wonder it is no longer possible to find a chariot. But before being taken apart, the chariot did exist as a composite and impermanent functional assemblage of pieces, and it was possible to drive with it. In fact, what made it a chariot was not just any of its parts or even all of them together but precisely their placement in relation to each other in such a way that the result becomes functional. In other words, what makes up a chariot are the appropriate causes and conditions. This is why no chariot can be found in any of its pieces, simply because the term "chariot" refers to their functional assemblage; in other words, it refers to a specific set of conditions.

The same holds for an individual. None of the five aggregates is the individual, and if it were possible to take these apart like the parts of a chariot, the individual would cease to exist. But as long as the five aggregates are related to each other in a functional assemblage, the individual exists as something composite and impermanent. As mentioned above, such individuals may well refer to themselves with terms like "I" and "my," which are not problematic as long as it remains clear that what is being referred to is composite and impermanent. The individual as a changing process, being devoid of anything permanent, does exist. This is precisely why teachings on karma and rebirth are applicable to such an individual.[129]

Two of the higher knowledges developed by the Buddha during the night of his awakening are recollection of his own past lives and the direct witnessing of others passing away and being reborn in accordance with their karma.[130] Although this is not explicitly stated in the texts, it seems fair to propose that witnessing his different identities in past lives would have led him to investigate what keeps these identities together such that as an individual now he can recollect those past experiences. The answer to this question is conditionality, evident particularly well on observing the passing away and rebirth of others. From this viewpoint, then, karma, as a specific instance of conditionality, is the litmus test for a proper understanding of not self. If these two are seen to contradict each other or be incompatible, the conclusion can be drawn that the understanding of not self requires revision.[131]

Reformulating the basic position in terms of emptiness and conditionality: the void of emptiness is full to the brim with causes and conditions. These causes and conditions are never being denied. What the teaching on the absence of a self denies is some sort of independent entity that is apart from causes and conditions, that exists on its own and is beyond change.

A helpful image for conveying the thrust of the teaching on not self takes the form of a mirror that we may grasp in order to see the reflection of our own face.[132] This can be taken to illustrate clinging to a sense of self, in particular the conceit "I am." Just as we will see the reflection of our own face only as long as we grasp the mirror and hold it up, in the same way the notion "I am" will only occur in a form that is tinged by conceit as long as there is clinging to a sense of self. Hence, the task is to drop the mirror. In the present context, such dropping has been considerably facilitated through the previous perception of infinite consciousness, due to which we are already accustomed to being less carried away by the contents of what the mirror reflects, having become more aware of the mirror itself. This of course makes it easier to let go of it.

Below I translate a Pāli verse that hopefully captures some of the key points regarding the teaching on not self. The prose introduction to this verse, which is the first in a set of three verses, contrasts what is commonly held to be true and false with the vision of awakened ones. This vision regards as false what the world in general believes to be true and considers to be true what others think to be false.[133]

See the world with its celestials,
Imagining a self in what is not self.
Entrenched in name-and-form,
It imagines that "this is true."

5. Summary

A practical implementation of the perception of nothingness as part of the gradual meditation on emptiness can conveniently employ one out of three approaches to the full attainment of nothingness delineated in another discourse that also relies on interrelating tranquility and insight, similar in this respect to the Smaller Discourse on Emptiness. The relevant approach proposed in this other discourse calls for the contemplation that "this is empty of a self and what belongs to a self."

The notion of a self that is being targeted here concerns a permanent entity. The doctrine of not self is grounded in the recognition of impermanence, together with the realization that what is impermanent is unable to provide lasting satisfaction. This is what the teaching on the absence of a self denies, nothing more and nothing less, namely the existence of something permanent that, due to being beyond change, can provide lasting satisfaction.

The repercussions of this teaching do not only apply to the cognitive belief that some such permanent entity exists but also concern emotionally held attitudes, such as appropriation and conceit. Although a stream-enterer is already beyond believing in the existence of a permanent self, it takes progressing all the way up to becoming an arahant to remove all traces of appropriation and conceit from the mind.

With later times an overstatement of the teaching on not self can manifest, in the form of asserting that an individual does not exist at all. In the case of a chariot, the idea is that, since it can be taken apart and none of the parts can be identified as the chariot, the conclusion can be drawn that there was no chariot in the first place. Yet, the term "chariot" refers to a functional assemblage of pieces that makes it possible to drive. If the chariot is taken apart, this functional assemblage has been destroyed. No wonder that a chariot can no longer be found. Before being taken apart, however, the chariot did exist as an impermanent assemblage of parts. That is, the term "chariot" refers to a specific set of causes and conditions. The same holds for an individual.

What the present step in the gradual meditation on emptiness targets is a permanent entity. Understood in this way, implementing the perception of nothingness is about there being nothing permanent rather than nothing at all, just as the teaching on not self is about there being no permanent self rather than nothing at all.

6. Practical Instructions

As earlier, practice of the present perception builds on the steps mentioned in the previous chapters. Based on having set our motivation, awareness can proceed via physical and mental seclusion to the perception of earth, then move through the other three elements up to infinite space, and then turn to consciousness, which by dint of having taken infinite space as its object has become infinite itself.

Similar to the case of the previous perceptions, there is a need to beware of taking things too literally and thereby missing the main point. Just as the perception of infinite space does not mean it is now possible to walk through walls, and just as the perception of infinite consciousness does not imply that nothing exists outside of the sphere of subjective cognition, so the absence of a self does not deny the reality of subjective experience. There is no problem in using words like "I" and "mine," as long as this takes place without conceit and attachment. The issue targeted here is the innate belief that there is a substantial and unchanging self or essence. This is the root cause of defilements, of conceit and clinging, which in the case of unawakened beings lurks behind all I-making and my-making.

What stands in place of the function, attributed by the unawakened mind to the self, is conditionality. Letting go of the misleading belief in a permanent self is precisely what enables a full appreciation of the process of causes and conditions that makes up subjective experience. The intention of the teaching on not self is certainly not to deny these but much rather to enable their recognition and understanding.

In actual practice the present step requires dropping the burden of the ego that can lurk at the background of the experience of infinite consciousness. Such dropping is particularly relevant to the case of consciousness, as its experience can only too easily lead to mistaken notions that there is something permanent in experience, that there is after all something that can be taken as a basis for the construction of notions of a self. Instead, consciousness is nothing but a process of being conscious that is impermanent through and through.

By way of illustration of the present step, the experience of infinite consciousness could be compared to holding up a glass of plain water against the sunlight. Despite it being plain water, closer inspection shows some minute particles floating around in the water. On applying a purifying filter, even these particles can be removed, and the water becomes completely clean. In the same way, the experience of infinite consciousness can be purified of any trace of selfing through applying the filter of the present perception. Compared to the shift from infinite space to infinite consciousness, the present progression is still subtler. At the same time, it shares with the previous perceptions that the main meditative task is one of recognition of an absence that is already there. Just as there is no need to fabricate space or consciousness, which just need to be recognized, similarly there is no need to construe the absence of a self. The self is a construct through and through; hence, it is by stopping construction that its deluding nature can be revealed and its absence fully recognized.

Throughout, emptiness is not something to be done but rather something to be understood and recognized. Hence, even a trace of straining in actual meditation practice is an indicator that something is not going quite in the right direction. Often enough, mere recognition of the attempt to become active when this is not at all required, in the sense that there is building up rather than letting go, can suffice to get back on track. Of course, as with all practices, the present step requires some time of familiarization before it can be executed with ease and naturalness. Nevertheless, from the outset it is helpful to keep an eye on excessive effort, which is one of the avenues for selfing to assert itself, by way of a sense of control. In a way applying much effort is natural, as we want to do our best to implement the meditative perception. Yet, such inspiration is best invested in an effortless effort, that is, in an effort to be rather than to do, to let go rather than to construe.

Progression through the two preceding perceptions provides substantial support for cultivating the present step in the gradual meditation on emptiness. The perception of infinite space undermines the spatial sense of selfhood; in fact, it is precisely this loss of a location for I-making and my-making that can trigger unease or even fear when we are not yet used to relating to our body as space. For the groundwork to be established in this way, it is particularly helpful to cultivate the perception of infinite space on its own for some time before shifting to infinite consciousness. The reason is that shifting too quickly, or even sidestepping the perception of infinite space and proceeding directly to infinite consciousness, can inadvertently strengthen the tendency of the mind to latch on to the latter by way of identification. The underlying pattern is a bit as if, on being forced to acknowledge that there is no support for selfing in the physical realm, the mind quickly shifts gear and tries to rely on consciousness as offering such support.

As already mentioned, consciousness is the one out of the five aggregates that is most easily reified and turned into a foundation for self-notions. For this very reason, the present step is of such importance, by way of purifying the sublime and profound experience of infinite consciousness of any trace of selfing. This purification is based on the groundwork done with the two preceding perceptions, which have first of all dissolved all material pegs for selfing and then shown consciousness to be of a boundless nature, beyond the boundaries that usually come with the average sense of an individual self. However, it is of course also possible to take precisely such a boundless and infinite consciousness as a self, to appropriate it and turn it into a building block for the conceit of being an accomplished meditator. For this reason, right now even that infinite consciousness needs to be thoroughly divested of any I-making and my-making.

In addition to the groundwork provided by the previous trajectory in the gradual meditation on emptiness, it can be quite helpful if the topic of not self is explored repeatedly in daily life. It is during daily life, particularly in challenging situations, that the tendency toward selfing can be clearly seen at work, as long as we are willing to dedicate the required time and mental space to notice it, even if only in retrospection. The clarity of understanding gained in this way can in turn inform the understanding of what is to be left behind at the present juncture in formal meditation.

Another and similarly relevant area of exploration is the occurrence of distractions during meditation. Such exploration builds on the foundation laid through the previous perception, which made it clear that the existence of thoughts is not in itself a problem, as long as there is a recognition of what is taking place. Building on the reassuring realization that successful meditation does not equate to having a thought-free mind, with the present perception the occurrence of thoughts can be turned into food for insight. This takes the form of first of all acknowledging that distractions and daydreams usually have some form of selfing at their core, which with maturing practice comes to be ever more clearly recognized. Moreover, the very purpose of such distractions and daydreams seems to be precisely to reassure the sense of self, which in spite of being only a construct does not want to be recognized as such. For this reason, as soon as there is silence in the mind, the sense of self struggles to raise its head in one way or another by introducing something that feels more palpably to be *mine* and hence reassures me that *I am* there. With this much recognized, a useful strategy can then be to turn to the thought with the inquiry: "Who?" The sense behind such an inquiry is to question ourselves: "Who is thinking here? Who is fantasizing?" Directly confronted with such an inquiry, what often happens is almost as if the thoughts become embarrassed on being asked for their credentials and thereby lose their momentum.

This strategy of direct inquiry builds on the work with distraction done with the previous two stages in the gradual meditation on emptiness. With the perception of infinite space, the recommended procedure is to learn to be at ease with thoughts by surrounding them with space. This reveals how much distracted thinking relies on a narrow state of mind in order to thrive. With the next stage of infinite consciousness, the occurrence of distraction can lead to turning toward the knowing part of the mind. This involves a shift from the ingrained tendency to get involved with the *what* of experience, in the sense of its content, by instead attending to its *how*, in the sense of its operational mechanisms. By turning our attention to the knowing part of experience, the thoughts lose their importance and are transformed into a tool for being with that which knows. With the present step, distracted thinking can become an integral part of the meditative experience—in the hope that I am not overstating my case—insofar as recognition of its occurrence provides an occasion for exploring and better understanding the way selfing builds up. The realization that all such distracted thinking is but a show, put up by the ego to defend itself, can have a remarkably transformative effect on our attitudes and outlooks.

For the sake of continuity of practice, the present perception can additionally be related to the breath. With each exhalation we can give particular emphasis to the empty nature of anything that could possibly be appropriated or clung to. The inhalation can serve to develop more emphasis on the absence of anything within that could justify the notion

of a self. In this way, the maxim for practice can become as follows: "No thing to own and no one to be." There is indeed nothing at all that deserves to be clung to through my-making or to be used to construct the conceit of I-making, as all that is there is thoroughly empty of a self and what belongs to a self.

The dropping of the burden of the ego turns out to be such a remarkable relief. This very experience of relief provides reassurance that this type of practice is not detrimental. To the contrary, the dropping of the burden of the ego is a gain rather than a loss; it improves our ability to function in the world rather than impairing it. Leaving behind selfing at the present juncture is particularly effective due to the preparatory work established through the previous perceptions, which enabled a gathering of the whole world of materiality into space and then a gathering together of everything experienced through the perception that all is in the mind.

Based on the groundwork provided in this way, all the outgrowths of the construction of experience are collected into a single container, as it were: the mind. From the subjective perspective, all appearances are but the creation of name-and-form, mirrored on consciousness. If consciousness is seen as thoroughly empty, the same inevitably applies to name-and-form and thus to all appearances, to anything manifesting in subjective experience. If the *presence* of experience is empty, its *content* must also be empty. In this way, with the present step it becomes possible to address the whole gamut of the drama of experience by depriving it of its foundation. This can be compared to tracing back the different outgrowths of a creeper until we finally put our hands on its main root, which has so far been hidden from sight. Having identified the main root makes any cutting through most efficient, which in the present case is a cutting through selfing with the inner sword of wisdom. In this way, the previous meditative trajectory ensures that such wielding of the sword of wisdom is maximally efficient.

Leaving behind selfing leaves behind a type of disturbance or weariness of which we may not have been fully aware previously. It is almost as if the inner space unnecessarily occupied by selfing now becomes free and can be utilized in more meaningful ways. A natural flourishing of the divine abodes, which are the other side of the coin of the realization of emptiness, is one of the most reliable signposts for genuine insight into not self.

By fully targeting the notion of a self, be it held cognitively or just as an instinctive assumption underlying self-referentiality, the present perception in a way complements the perception of earth. The perception of earth can make a substantial contribution to overcoming the notion of being a separate self that is set apart from the rest of the world. In this way, a circular pattern can be discerned: just as the perception of infinite consciousness complements the perception of infinite space, the two being in a way sides of the same coin, the perception that follows this pair (nothingness) complements the perception that precedes them (earth). The same pattern continues, as the next perception of signlessness, in the sense of the absence of all signs, complements the perception of seclusion, which is about a more specific type of absence. Understood in this way, the overall meditative trajectory can be seen to involve a circular dimension alongside its evident linear progression.

Each step in this linear and at the same time circular meditative development requires proceeding from a more active implementation of the meditative perception to a more passive abiding in the resultant realization. Similar to the case of the divine abodes (see above p. 21), each step calls for a shift from doing to being. There is nothing wrong if the initial period of practice of each step appears a bit conceptual and its implications do not quite sink in. This is only to be expected. But with patient perseverance, the notion of emptiness relevant to each step becomes more embodied, more something that is naturally present rather than needing to be intentionally aroused. In a way, the effort to contemplate the world as empty becomes increasingly effortless, and events in the world are increasingly experienced as manifestations of emptiness. Whatever appears in our field of cognition is but an expression of emptiness, and any problem or challenge encountered is but an opportunity to plunge deeper into emptiness. In this way, the presence of an absence—in the present case the absence of a self—stands out naturally as the most prominent feature of any experience, and a profound inner silence prevails over all the noise in the world.

The silent freedom from the burden of the ego also comprises the very perception of nothingness itself. This is in keeping with a recurrent pattern in the instructions, which point out the disturbance or weari-

ness left behind and immediately add that the very perception that has achieved this much is at the same time a disturbance or weariness that is still present. Although the present perception is empty of what has been left behind, which in the present case are the subject-object duality and selfing, it is not empty of the very perception that has accomplished this. A clear awareness that the present perception is not yet the supreme emptiness, however powerful it may be, makes abiding in it particularly beneficial. Coming out of the formal meditation session, the backward tour falls into place by returning to infinite consciousness, infinite space, earth, and seclusion, once again noting how in this way the experience becomes gradually coarser, more on the side of disturbances and weariness. The concluding point remains sharing our merits.

As far as daily-life applications are concerned, there is of course no end to the potential benefits to be expected from implementing the maxim that "this is empty of a self and what belongs to a self." Dropping the burden of selfing and ego makes life just so much more easeful for ourselves and all those with whom we come into contact. The clear understanding that this modality of nothingness does not affirm that there is nothing at all is crucial here, as it shows that personal responsibility and dedication to important issues like social justice, etc., are definitely not being called into question. To the contrary, they can become substantially more effective to the degree to which self-centeredness has been diminished. Actualizing this potential simply requires dropping the mirror of conceit. This is to let go of the assumption that my sense of "I" should serve as the epicenter around which the whole world revolves, with everyone else having to cater to the likes and dislikes of this epicenter. Although this assumption may not always manifest in the glaring manner just described, self-referentiality is a fairly continuous element of unawakened experience. It can be redressed by simply noting such self-referentiality with mindfulness, then letting go of it, and then noting how much more agreeable everything becomes, how much more effectively any task can be performed, once the epicenter of the ego has been dropped.

Besides offering an important exploration ground for noticing patterns of selfing, daily life also provides an important training ground for letting go of these. Walking meditation can be done without any sense of

I and mine in relation to the walking: Walking without a walker, so to say. Breathing without a breather, speaking without a speaker, and so on. There is no end to the opportunities to explore how much more harmonious and efficient we can become just through the simple step of dropping the burden of the ego. In other words, we learn to be in the present moment without owning even that present moment.

Whenever defilements arise, the strategy of non-identification shows its true worth. It offers an approach to dealing with defilements that can be compared to the martial art *tàijí quán* (popularly known as "tai chi"). Rather than struggle, we simply get out of the way in a manner that preserves inner balance and lets the energy of defilements charge by and disperse, due to not finding a place to land. That is, in a way, the key potential of implementing the teaching on not self: leaving defilements no place to land.

VII. Signlessness

Again, Ānanda, not attending to the perception of the sphere of <infinite consciousness> and not attending to the perception of the sphere of <nothingness>, a monastic attends to oneness in dependence on signless concentration of the mind. Their mind enters upon, is pleased with, settles on, and is devoted to the signless concentration of the mind.

They understand like this: "Whatever disturbances there could be in dependence on <the perception of the sphere of infinite consciousness>, these are not present here. Whatever disturbances there could be in dependence on <the perception of the sphere of nothingness>, these are not present here. There is just this remainder of disturbance, namely the oneness in dependence on <the signless concentration of the mind>."

They understand: "This perceptual range is empty of <the perception of the sphere of infinite consciousness>"; and they understand: "This perceptual range is empty of <the perception of the sphere of nothingness>. There is just this non-emptiness, namely the oneness in dependence on <the signless concentration of the mind>."

Thus, they contemplate it as empty of what is indeed not there, and they understand that what remains there is still present: "It is there." Ānanda, like this there also comes to be for them this genuine, undistorted, and purified entry into emptiness.[134]

1. The Progression up to Signlessness

The pointed brackets in the extract translated above are meant to mark emendations. These are required because the Pāli version appears to have suffered from transmission errors.[135] One of these involves taking up the attainment of neither-perception-nor-nonperception before coming to signless concentration. This is unexpected, since the meditative trajectory is throughout based on working with perceptions. In contrast, the attainment of neither-perception-nor-nonperception, as its very name indicates, is a condition where perception becomes attenuated to the point that it is no longer possible to say that one is fully perceptive, yet at the same time one is also not without perception. Judging from what can be gleaned from other discourses, the attainment of neither-perception-nor-nonperception does not fit the present context particularly well.[136]

Another problem in the Pāli version is that it takes up signless concentration twice, both times mentioning a leaving behind of the same disturbance. This does not fit with what is clearly a description of progressive stages of meditation, each of which results in a deepening of letting go. Thus it seems that at some stage in oral transmission the passage on signless concentration was accidentally doubled, and some unclarity about the meditative progression at the present juncture led to supplementing the attainment of neither-perception-nor-nonperception, in line with the usual inclusion of this attainment in other contexts that mention the previous three immaterial spheres of infinite space, infinite consciousness, and nothingness.

The Chinese and Tibetan parallels do not mention the attainment of neither-perception-nor-nonperception and take up signlessness only once, with the minor difference that the Tibetan version uses the term "signless element" instead of "signless concentration."[137] Such signlessness is then also the disturbance or non-emptiness left at this juncture. The emendations applied above to the Pāli version follow this mode of presentation in the Chinese and Tibetan parallels.

2. The Notion of Signlessness

The basic sense of the "sign" (Pāli and Sanskrit: *nimitta*) is the characteristic mark of something, which enables perception to recognize what that something is. Due to its function to *cause* the arising of a memory or association, the term "sign" can at times convey a plain *causal* nuance.[138] Signlessness in turn is an intentional abstaining from taking up any sign, a deliberate ignoring of the signposts that experience offers for the purposes of recognition and mental association, a refusal to construct meaning out of the available data provided by the senses.

The standard description of signless concentration in the early discourses stipulates two conditions for its attainment: "not giving attention to any sign" and "giving attention to the signless element."[139] The two conditions mentioned in this way complement each other. Since attention is present in any state of mind, once it does not take up any sign, there is a need to explain what it does instead, which in the present case is giving attention to their absence. This appears to be what the "signless element" stands for. The explicit mention of this second condition clarifies that signless concentration differs from the attainment of neither-perception-nor-nonperception, for example, or else from just being unconscious. The meditative cultivation of signlessness does not issue in a state where the taking up of signs is in principle impossible, because perception has become partially or completely dysfunctional. Perception remains fully functional but is deprived of its usual food, so to say, as the practitioner maintains the conscious resolve not to pick up any sign.

The type of concentration under discussion here is devoid of a circumscribed object to focus on, thereby partaking of the nature of the previous steps. As mentioned earlier, cultivating these perceptions requires mindfulness more than a concentrative focus. Leading the mind into a calm abiding, without relying on something to focus on, may at first appear challenging for those who are accustomed to employing a clearly circumscribed object on which to concentrate. However, the cultivation of "concentration," *samādhi*, or perhaps better "mental composure" or "collectedness," is not confined to such focusing on a circumscribed object. It can also take place in a quite different manner, as is the case for the present and the two preceding steps.

A particularly helpful indication in this respect can be found in a description of the faculty (*indriya*) of *samādhi* given in some Pāli discourses, although this description is not found in the respective parallels. This definition of the faculty of concentration provides the following indication: "having made letting go the basis, one will gain concentration and will gain unification of the mind."[140] The idea of letting go would be particularly pertinent to the present type of *samādhi*, which requires letting go of all signs.

3. Sense Restraint

Abiding in signlessness can best be cultivated as the outcome of a gradual process of meditative training in relation to signs. The first and foundational stage here is sense restraint. Such a form of practice is particularly apt for daily-life situations. The main task is to establish sufficient mindfulness to realize when anything that happens at one sense door or the other leads to unwholesome reactivity in the mind, which usually takes the form of likes and dislikes. The instructions for such sense restraint speak quite specifically of avoiding the tendency to *grasp* the sign, to cling to it, which then usually leads over to further associations and elaborations in the realm of the mind.[141] Sensual desire, anger, and delusion can operate as makers of signs in this way.[142] These three root defilements can become makers of signs in the sense that *grasping* some feature of what is being perceived at any of the sense doors can serve as a trigger for their arising.

Building on previous meditative training, it becomes increasingly easy to notice when the mind enters into a defiled condition. Such noticing provides the feedback that there is an urgent need to let go of the sign responsible for arousing a defilement, together with the various associations and proliferations this tends to call up.

When this approach is implemented successfully, the brief arising of a defilement and its subsequent swift quelling can become a powerful lesson in how the sign can impact the mind. Practicing in this way reveals the conditionality of the perceptual process and shows the degree to which the untrained mind can become a hapless victim of signs, something that advertising in contemporary society is well aware of and exploits in a range of different manners. Understood in this way, already this first stage of working with signs can result in a palpable experience of inner freedom, by way of skillfully avoiding that the mind takes up signs connected with defilements and thereby enters into bondage and misery.

4. Bare Awareness

Building on the groundwork in meditative training with signs laid through sense restraint, a further stage in working with signs can take the form of bare awareness. The basic practice of bare awareness requires a good foundation in being well established in mindfulness. When anything comes up at any sense door, this should then be received in its bare condition of sensory information, after which the mind just remains still. There is thus a pause after the first input has been registered, rather than moving onward and becoming involved with various associations and proliferations.

Hearing a sound can provide a convenient illustration, already explored above in relation to the perception of infinite consciousness (see p. 86). The normal way of reacting to hearing a sound is to try to locate its source and ascertain its import. To do so is of course natural as a survival strategy inherited from early stages in the development of human beings. For a Neanderthal living out in the wilds, quickness in locating the direction from which a sound arrived and in understanding what it meant was a matter of ensuring survival. However, nowadays, this type of reaction is not always necessary. Instead of requiring invariably a quick reaction on the spot, there is ample room for cultivating bare awareness. In the case of a sound, then, the task would be to stay with the ear sense door, as it were. Staying with the ear sense door, we are staying with the reception of the sound, rather than reaching out mentally to become involved with the sound as an object occurring somewhere externally.

A net result of such staying with the ear (or any other sense door) can take the form of placing less emphasis on objects as things out there and instead giving more prominence to the process of hearing. This is rather significant, since it implies a shift toward a more process-oriented way of experiencing. A fundamental problem with signs is that, in order to facilitate recognition, the mind tends to focus on signs that are least affected by change. For the purpose of recognizing another person, for example, it will not be particularly useful if we store in mind signs related to their clothing, since on the next occasion of meeting them, chances are high that they will be wearing different clothing. Even hairstyle is not a safe guide. Instead, features less amenable to change commend themselves for being taken up as the sign for recognition. As a result of this basic pattern, however, there is an implicit assumption of permanency built into the very process of perception, through the taking up of signs and our resultant success in recognition and identification. In a way, every successful instance of recognizing and identifying not only provides positive feedback regarding our ability in taking up signs, showing that perception is working well, but also supports the tacit impression that there must be something permanent beneath changing phenomena.

Bare awareness can help to counter this pattern by divesting the apparently quite solid external objects, perceived from the viewpoint of their most permanent features, of their presumed importance. Instead, what really counts is the process of seeing, hearing, smelling, tasting, and touching. The role of the sense door becomes more prominent in this way, ousting the previous, one-sided emphasis on the sense object as the one and all of sensory experience.

A particularly remarkable case of such practice involves the story of the non-Buddhist practitioner Bāhiya, who became an arahant/arhat right on the spot after receiving the following instruction at what was his first encounter with Buddhist teachings:[143]

> Therefore, Bāhiya, you should train yourself here like this: in what is seen there will be just what is seen, in what is heard there will be just what is heard, in what is sensed there will be just what is sensed, in what is cognized there will be just what is cognized. Bāhiya, you should train yourself thus.

> Bāhiya, when for you in what is seen there will be just what is seen, in what is heard there will be just what is heard, in what is sensed there will be just what is sensed, in what is cognized there will be just what is cognized, then, Bāhiya, you will not be thereby (*na tena*). Bāhiya, when you will not be thereby, then, Bāhiya, you will not be therein (*na tattha*). Bāhiya, when you will not be therein, then, Bāhiya, you will be neither here, nor beyond, nor between the two. Just this is the end of *dukkha*.

Without intending to dismiss alternative modes of interpretation, from a practical perspective the above passage can be taken to convey that, with bare awareness at each sense door, the thingness of objects dissolves and we are no longer carried away by the content of what is being experienced: "not thereby." Instead of all attention being on things out there as the objects of experience, there is a growing awareness of the process character of experience. With such a shift in perspective, not only the objects but also the subject begin to fade away, in the sense of the innate assumption that there is an "I" that forms the epicenter of any experience and somehow is in control of it all: "not therein." Once there is no longer a "thereby" or a "therein," we no longer hold on to any aspect of experience and no longer become established on it in any way: "neither here, nor beyond, nor between the two." The profound letting go that can result from such practice evidently has a remarkable liberating potential. Although in the case of Bāhiya this much was already enough, a further step to actualize this liberating potential can be taken by cultivating signlessness.

5. Abiding in Signlessness

Working with the sign at the level of sense restraint will usually take place during daily-life experiences. Of course, in principle the same can also happen in formal meditation, such as when, for example, suddenly a loud noise occurs and an effort is needed to avoid grasping the sign of anger and irritation. But in principle the main avenue for working with sense restraint is when being outside of formal meditation and in a situation where anything can happen at the sense doors. The next level of working with signs, bare awareness, is sometimes possible in such situations, although this only makes sense when being in a relatively safe and secure environment, such as, for example, doing walking meditation during a retreat. When being out in the world, there is a constant need to locate sound and understand its implications rapidly, such as when crossing a road and hearing the noise of a truck approaching at high speed. In such a situation, bare awareness would not be an appropriate choice. In sum, bare awareness is more easily applied during formal meditation practice.

Abiding in signlessness in turn can only really be implemented in a sustained manner during formal sitting meditation. Once there is no taking up of signs, perception no longer functions fully, wherefore it would be difficult even to do walking meditation in that condition. This is not to deny that there can be a brief flash of signlessness in various situations. But with continuous abiding in signlessness the construction of experience is dismantled to an extent that is only fully possible when being in a situation where, for the time being, nothing needs to be done at the bodily level.

This does not imply that signless concentration relies on suppressing some part of experience in any way. When we sit in formal meditation and cultivate signlessness, sounds will sooner or later occur. Hearing sounds is not being repressed, as any such activity would run counter to the very practice of thoroughly letting go. However, at the same time any sound will also not be recognized for what it is, simply because any such identification requires taking up a sign and therefore also runs counter to the very practice of signlessness.

The cultivation of signlessness itself calls for dropping whatever sign the mind had just been involved with at present, followed by not taking up any other sign. Such a meditative procedure can be viewed as a practical implementation of the dictum that all the teachings, however sublime, are merely a raft for the purpose of crossing over.[144] There comes a time when even the raft needs to be left behind in order to be able to complete the journey.

The image of a raft that eventually needs to be relinquished fits the progression of the gradual meditation on emptiness particularly well. Each of its individual steps relies on letting go of the preceding perception. The raft of nothingness, which has enabled transcending all self-referentiality in relation to infinite consciousness, in turn also needs to be left behind. The very sword of wisdom, so powerfully effective in cutting through conceit and appropriation, also needs to be abandoned. Even the resultant experience of signlessness, which involves such a thorough letting go, in turn is also just a raft that eventually needs to be left behind. I will return to this need in the next chapter.

The experience resulting from letting go of any sign, and from not taking up any other sign, has something in common with other practices of concentration (*samādhi*), in particular a natural stillness at the bodily level, absence of any distraction, and mental unification. However, this takes place without any reference point whatsoever. Such practice thus goes further than the cultivation of infinite space and infinite consciousness, discussed in previous chapters. Already the cultivation of these types of calm abiding requires foregoing any circumscribed focus, instead of which the infinitude of space or of consciousness as a theme or topic provides the only available support for establishing collectedness of the mind. With signlessness, even such a theme or topic is no longer available, and the meditative experience becomes one of total and absolute absence. As soon as the mind reaches out for anything to do, and thus for a sign, we immediately need to let go then and there in order to be able to continue abiding in the absence of any signs.

Helpful information for such abiding can be gathered from a Pāli passage that describes a particular type of concentration, which the Chinese parallel indicates to be indeed signless concentration. The Pāli description offers the following indications:[145]

> Not leaning forward and not leaning backward, concentration is reached without exertion by holding in check and restraining. Through being freed, one is stable; through being stable, one is contented; and through being contented, one is not agitated.

The first part points to a need for balance. Out of various possible explanations of the significance of not leaning forward or backward, to my mind a particularly appealing interpretation takes this to refer to having no negativity toward signs, such as feeling repulsion toward them, and also not to arouse clinging to their absence, that is, to the signless element.[146] This conveniently illustrates the best attitude for a cultivation of signlessness. Although there is a clear and intentional decision to let go of any sign, the absence of such leaning forward or backward facilitates continuity in abiding. If a sign should arise, any reaction by way of negativity toward the sign or clinging to the absence of the sign would amplify the distraction. Swiftly letting go of the sign is most easily achieved if no emotional reactivity is involved. In addition to resulting in higher efficiency, the absence of negativity and clinging also conveniently feeds into the main attitude that informs the whole practice: letting go.

A helpful image can be the process of deciduous trees shedding their leaves in autumn. Although this process involves an active shedding, this is not a forceful act but just a quiet and gentle shedding of what for the time being is of no further use. Similarly, abiding in signlessness can just be a quiet letting go, without aversion toward what is being dropped and without latching on to the resultant absence. Just softly and gently letting go. The mind is in a way suspended without anything to do.

This can at times be experienced as a kind of uninvolved hovering or a deep resting or a free floating, although it is important to avoid using any of these images to construct a sign of what signless meditation is about and then latching on to that sign. The images of uninvolved hovering, deep resting, and free floating are only crutches meant to convey the direction in which practice can evolve; they should be handled with care to avoid mistaking the finger that points at the moon for being the moon itself.

Throughout our abiding in signlessness, making an effort would result in taking up signs, hence the reference in the passage translated above to the absence of any exertion, any holding in check or restraining. The task is not to do, construct, or fabricate. This is a form of meditation that no longer calls for an active cultivation (*bhāvanā*) but only takes the form of a passive abiding in letting go.

The very freedom from any reference point or prop to maintain mental composure, which at first can make abiding in signlessness quite challenging, with familiarity and growing expertise in avoiding distractions can turn into a source of mental stability. A key feature here is contentment. Precisely because of being contented with the absence of anything happening in the mind, it becomes easier to continue to abide in such absence. Any reaching out for a sign would imply a lack of contentment and a subtle wish for something else that is more entertaining. Free from such wishes and endowed with such freedom, mental stability, and contentment, the mind cannot be agitated anymore. Just a profound sense of stillness and quietude remains, free from even a trace of effort and, precisely for that reason, being still and quiet. The experience of such mental freedom through abiding in signlessness can perhaps best be illustrated with the example of birds freely flying in the sky without leaving any track behind:[147]

> Whose pasture is empty
> And signless liberation:
> Their track is hard to trace,
> Like that of birds in the sky.

6. Summary

The instructions for the present step in the Pāli version appear to have suffered from errors during transmission, which can be rectified with the help of the Chinese and Tibetan parallels. These indicate that practice can proceed from the perception of nothingness directly to signlessness (rather than to neither-perception-nor-nonperception).

Attending to signlessness requires letting go of those marks and characteristics with the help of which we recognize and identify. The absence of any such sign can serve as the reference point for concentration. This results in a modality of practice that not only does not focus on a circumscribed object but also does not rely on any other theme or topic. What is required here is a mindful presence with a total absence, namely the complete absence of any sign. This type of practice builds on the undercurrent of attending to specific types of absence with the preceding steps, bringing them to a culmination point.

Working with signs is a gradual process and can take place at different levels. A basic and more active type of training can be the cultivation of sense restraint. This calls for mindful recognition when we grasp a sign that is about to trigger (or else has just triggered) the arising of a defilement in the mind.

Another and more sophisticated way of working with signs is bare awareness. This requires remaining mindfully present with whatever occurs at any of the sense doors without further elaborations. The case of the non-Buddhist practitioner Bāhiya shows the transformative potential of such practice.

Cultivating signless concentration in turn is still more sophisticated; it requires foregoing any type of recognition or identification. In a way, cultivating signlessness is a stepping back from wanting to make sense of things and instead resting with the bare process of experiencing. The presently arisen sign is dropped, after which the mind does not take up any other sign and just abides in the total absence of signs. Without repulsion toward signs or attachment to their absence, the mind learns to find stability in the very freedom from actively doing, constructing, and fabricating. The effortless effort of not participating in the usual activities of the mind relies on being contented with the most total absence possible within the realm of what is conditioned.

7. Practical Instructions

The cultivation of signlessness in a way completes a meditative trajectory that has its starting point in the introduction of the notion of absence through perception of the forest. The trajectory of recognizing what is absent and stepping out of the ingrained tendency to pay attention only to what is present comes to a culmination point with signlessness. From the viewpoint of an actual practice of the present step, it can be quite useful if we pay deliberate attention to the absence of those signs that are being left behind with each of the steps in the gradual meditation on emptiness. In other words, the recommendation is to proceed through the perceptual progression from the forest to nothingness, with an emphasis on leaving behind specific signs.

Thus, based on having formulated our motivation and attended to physical and mental seclusion as representative of the absence of the signs of physical and mental disturbances, with the perception of earth the signs that usually serve to discriminate individual instances of matter are left behind. In this way, signs causally related to the creation of dualistic contrasts are overcome. Next in line is the very sign of earth as solidity that has facilitated stepping out of dualistic contrasts. This can be deconstructed by bringing in the other elements as a way of illustrating that the solidity of earth is not something that exists independently in its own right. Eventually all of solidity, internally and externally, dissolves into space.

The sign of infinite space that has enabled this step is the one to be left behind with the next step, whereby the signs of all objects are left behind, such that only the cognizing subject remains. In this way, all external signs come to be encompassed by the internal dimension of experience, by way of being cognized in the mind. The emphasis on the role played by the experiencing subject, as a natural result of this progression, immediately comes up for deconstruction with the next step. At this point, all the signs related to I-making and my-making are to be dropped for good. In other words, after objects had to exit the scene, now the subject is asked to do the same. In this way, the foundation has been prepared for letting go of all signs completely with the present step. Viewing the meditative progression from the perspective of the gradual elimination of signs in this way reveals particularly well that all of this is not about getting or attaining something but about shedding something; it is about letting go.

At this point, after the perception of infinite consciousness has in a way gathered the whole world of experience into a single container, and after the perception of nothingness has wielded the sword of wisdom to cut through the tendrils of selfing at the very root of the world of experience, now even that sword of wisdom is to be relinquished. The main task is to let go of signs as completely as possible and keep letting go of them as soon as the mind begins to reach out for one. In a way, after the absence of any ownership of subjective experience has been established with the previous perception of nothingness, now even any appropriation of signs needs to be left behind. Expressed in a different way, after relinquishing first the objects of experience and then the subject of experience, now the usual interaction between these two—the middle or the in-between—also is to be given up. The approach to be adopted for this purpose could perhaps be encapsulated in this way:

> Mind at rest: let it be!
> Mind moves: let go!

Formal meditation continues by way of surfing on the wave of emptiness that has been generated through the earlier perceptions. Having earlier let go of the object of meditation and then of the subject of meditation, now even the idea of actively meditating has been relinquished. Practice continues on its own accord, moving beyond the realm of language and concepts. In a way, it is all about just sitting silently and allowing the emptiness of the present moment to wash away any-"thing" else. Observation of the breath in support of abiding in signlessness is no longer really possible, as discerning between inhalations and exhalations would involve taking up signs.

As an outdoor type of practice to complement formal sitting, appropriate when being in a situation where we have nothing to do and can fully relax, it can be helpful to look up at the sky. Next, we quickly move through the preceding three perceptions by apprehending the infinite nature of the space of the sky, allowing the cognizing consciousness to become similarly vast, and dropping any self-referentiality. Then we just relax and wait for the mind to take up any sign, ready to let go of it as soon as this is noticed. Inspiration for such practice can be gained from the image in the verse translated earlier that illustrates the nature of signlessness with the example of birds in the sky. In the same way, by dropping the taking up of signs, we leave no trace behind and experience freedom comparable to a bird in the sky.

The meditative progress undertaken up to this point can be related to the Bāhiya instruction. The attitude that can come to pervade daily life due to cultivation of the perceptions of earth and of infinite space, together with the resultant freedom from being strongly driven by likes and dislikes, could be matched to the first part of the instruction. This first part describes training in such a way that in what is seen, heard, sensed, and cognized there will be just what is seen, heard, sensed, and cognized. The insight gained through the perceptions of earth and infinite space makes it increasingly easy to remain with the actual experience rather than becoming overwhelmed by associations, evaluations, and reactivity triggered by what is seen, heard, sensed, and cognized.

Building on this level of practice, with the perception of infinite consciousness and its implication as a dropping of any concern with objects, naturally we are less easily carried away by those objects. As a result of that, we are "not thereby." This comes about in particular through the growing understanding that the real source of all experiences is the mind. Diminishing selfing through the perception of nothingness then can be related to the next aspect of the Bāhiya instruction, according to which we are "not therein." It is precisely the tendency toward selfing, the presence of conceit and clinging through appropriation, that leads to being established "therein." In the absence of these, and due to no longer being carried away by what is seen, heard, sensed, and cognized, we no longer feel a need to establish a subject of such seeing, hearing, sensing, and cognizing by somehow affirming an "I" that is therein.

In line with these same correlations, signlessness would then find its counterpart in being "neither here, nor beyond, nor between the two." In fact, this final part of the instruction to Bāhiya can be taken as an additional inspiration for abiding in signlessness, which is free not only from leaning forward or backward but also from a here, a beyond, or an in-between the two.

Whenever the time has come to conclude the abiding in signlessness, the reverse progression falls into place, which could again come with an emphasis on noting the signs that are now being taken up: the sign of not self, the sign of infinite consciousness, the sign of infinite space, the sign of earth, and the sign of the forest, followed by sharing our merits.

A direct application of abiding in signlessness to daily life is not really feasible, simply because it requires non-attention to any signs. Therefore, any attention to something that is present or happening implies that the condition of total absence has been left, even if only briefly. Instead of signlessness itself, sense restraint and bare awareness would be the practices to opt for in situations outside of formal meditation practice.

An example for working with signs in this way, in combination with the perception of infinite space as an additional tool for facing a challenging situation, can take the following form: A first step can be noticing briefly the space between us and the person(s) experienced as challenging or even aggressive. Such noting enables a broadening of the mind that naturally allows more room for understanding where the other(s) are coming from. Based on diminishing the inner space usually occupied by selfing, a specific modality of sense restraint can take the form of watching out for any strong latching on to signs, especially signs loaded with biased evaluations, in the understanding that this only makes things more difficult.

Although signlessness itself is not a practice for daily life, during any activity the taking up of signs can be observed and better understood, which will in turn foster the ability to drop these in formal meditation. Moreover, the cultivation of signlessness in formal meditation can have a rather significant impact by increasing awareness of the constructed nature of experience. This can have a remarkable impact on daily-life activities, by substantially diminishing conceptual proliferation. When we have seen through the construction of experience, we will no longer firmly believe the various dramas and stories our mind can create. Although complete freedom from conceptual proliferation requires proceeding further to full awakening, familiarity with signlessness in formal meditation will reduce the degree to which anything that happens, however challenging it may be, reverberates in the mind. The tendency to replay dramas and compose increasingly detailed auto-commentaries on these can no longer thrive as before, as it is being deprived of much of its foundation. In this way, there is ample scope to work with signs in daily life in order to be less easily carried away by what is happening, based on awareness of the constructed nature of the drama of experience.

VIII. Nirvana

They understand like this: "This signless concentration of the mind is also constructed and produced by volition, but whatever is constructed and produced by volition, that is impermanent and of a nature to cease"; [this] they understand.

Knowing like this and seeing like this, their mind is liberated from the influx of sensuality, their mind is liberated from the influx of becoming, and their mind is liberated from the influx of ignorance. On being liberated, there is the knowledge of it being "liberated," and they understand: "Birth is extinct, the holy life has been lived, what had to be done has been done, there is no further of this present state of being."

They understand like this: "Whatever disturbances there could be in dependence on the influx of sensuality, these are not present here. Whatever disturbances there could be in dependence on the influx of becoming, these are not present here. Whatever disturbances there could be in dependence on the influx of ignorance, these are not present here. There is just this remainder of disturbance, namely that of the six sense spheres in dependence on this body and conditioned by life."

They understand: "This perceptual range is empty of the influx of sensuality"; they understand: "This perceptual range is empty of the influx of becoming"; and they understand: "This perceptual range is empty of the influx of ignorance. There is just this non-emptiness, namely that of the six sense spheres in dependence on this body and conditioned by life."

Thus, they contemplate it as empty of what is indeed not there, and they understand that what remains there is still present: "It is there." Ānanda, like this there comes to be for them this genuine, undistorted, purified, supreme, and unsurpassed entry into emptiness.

Ānanda, whatever recluses and brahmins in the bygone past also abided having indeed attained purified, supreme, and unsurpassed emptiness, they all abided having attained this very purified, supreme, and unsurpassed emptiness. Ānanda, whatever recluses and brahmins in the distant future will also abide having indeed attained purified, supreme, and unsurpassed emptiness, they all will abide having attained this very purified, supreme, and unsurpassed emptiness. Ānanda, whatever recluses and brahmins in the present also abide having indeed attained purified, supreme, and unsurpassed emptiness, they all abide having attained this very purified, supreme, and unsurpassed emptiness.

Therefore, Ānanda, you should indeed train like this: "We shall abide having attained purified, supreme, and unsurpassed emptiness."[148]

1. Supreme Emptiness

The above passage presents the supreme in matters of emptiness: the freedom gained by emptying the mind of all defilements. At this stage, the gradual progression through various temporary experiences of emptiness culminates in making the emptiness described above become an enduring character trait of the practitioner.

This can be related to a point made in the first chapter in regard to the cultivation of the divine abodes (see above p. 21), in particular the recommendation to shift from doing, in the sense of an active arousal of a divine abode, to just being, in the sense of effortless abiding. The same type of shift is of continuous relevance to the gradual progression in emptiness, where each step can be seen as an invitation to proceed gradually toward an effortless embodying of the central insight on emptiness that forms the respective main theme. Such effortless embodying then reaches a climax when the mind has become emptied of defilements.

The climax under discussion is beyond meditation, in a way, as this type of emptiness no longer requires further cultivation in order to be maintained. Moreover, it is also beyond meditation in the sense that the breakthrough to awakening that effectuates the eradication of defilements cannot be made to happen through meditative efforts. Meditation prepares the ground by gradually maturing the mind in such a way that this breakthrough can take place in principle. Yet, the breakthrough itself is not something directly produced by meditation. It requires the most thorough letting go possible, which implies also a letting go of the activity of meditating, at least for that moment.[149] Holding on to anything, even if it is just the practice of meditation, would risk preventing the event of awakening from taking place.

In addition to preparing the ground for this event, for one who has reached this acme of emptiness, meditation is the most adequate expression of a genuine realization of emptiness. Even after his awakening, the Buddha is on record for having continued to adopt a meditative lifestyle of resorting to seclusion, which for him constituted an appropriate way of living and at the same time served as an expression of his compassion, presumably in the sense of setting an example for others.[150] A realization of the "supreme and unsurpassed" peak of emptiness also impacts daily life, as it turns the practice of an embodied mindfulness that remains free from desire, dejection, and unwholesome states—the first exercise mentioned in the first chapter (see above p. 5)—into a natural condition effortlessly maintained with uninterrupted continuity.

According to the Pāli version translated above, those who have gained realization of supreme emptiness are recluses and brahmins, whereas the parallels instead speak of Tathāgatas.[151] The term Tathāgata, which can be translated as "Thus gone one," stands for a fully awakened one. In its usage in the early discourses, at times the term designates specifically the Buddha and at other times it stands for a Buddha and his arahant disciples. According to the Pāli commentary, in the present case the Pāli version's reference to "recluses and brahmins" carries a closely corresponding sense, as it indeed refers to Buddhas and their disciples.[152] The Chinese and Tibetan versions of the part of the above statement about abiding in emptiness in the *present* time explicitly indicates that this refers to the Buddha himself. This thereby conveniently brings the discourse to a closure by relating the peak of its exposition back to the topic on which it started, namely the Buddha's own abiding in emptiness. On following the Pāli commentary, the same interrelation would also be relevant for the Pāli presentation.

On this reading, the preceding steps in the gradual meditation on emptiness can be understood as presenting one particular approach for following in the footsteps of the Buddha by way of gradually approaching and eventually accomplishing the supreme emptiness of the mind in the form of a total absence of defilements. Needless to say, this is not a case of completely emulating him in this respect, as he accomplished the feat of reaching such emptiness without relying on the guidance of a fully awakened teacher. Nevertheless, a thorough implementation of the instructions in this discourse can be expected to lead to the same basic condition of unshakable mental freedom.

The early discourses regularly refer to such unshakable mental freedom in terms of the eradication of the influxes (Pāli: *āsava*; Sanskrit: *āśrava* or *āsrava*), sometimes alternatively translated as "taints." The basic idea underlying the early Buddhist usage of this term is to designate three conditions whose corrupting influence on the mind is responsible for keeping us in bondage to the cycle of births and deaths. This differs from employments of the same term in other ancient Indian traditions, where it can refer to a material inflow as the result of karma.[153] Instead, the idea here is to point to a psychological type of influence in the form of sensuality, representative of desire for sensual gratification; becoming, in the sense of an inclination toward being reborn and its result in coming into existence; and ignorance, the main culprit for any form of bondage and for this reason the first link in the standard presentation of the dependent arising of *dukkha/duḥkha*.

To some extent, the preceding meditative trajectory can be taken to offer distinct contributions to the eradication of each of these three influxes. The perceptions of earth, infinite space, and infinite consciousness can be understood to offer such a contribution in particular in relation to the first influx of sensuality. The insight into the nature of material things, possible through the perceptions of earth and infinite space, can thoroughly undermine concern with the objects of sensuality. This has its complement in the realization of the degree to which the mind manufactures experience as a whole, which reveals the dream-like nature of all sensual indulgence. The perception of nothingness, here understood to refer in particular to insight into not self, deconstructs the central peg and foundation for any craving for becoming. This has its complement in meditation on signlessness, which can help letting go of the habitual drive of continuously reaching out for what is next, of leaning toward the future. At the same time, a proper practice of each of these perceptions of course undermines ignorance, a trajectory that will be brought to its successful conclusion with the realization of Nirvana.

2. The Four Noble Truths

The realization of Nirvana is central for what according to tradition was the first teaching given by the recently awakened Buddha: the four noble truths. This scheme points directly at what is needed to solve the central problem of *dukkha/duḥkha*. The basic diagnostic pattern underlying this scheme is as follows:

disease: *dukkha/duḥkha*
pathogen: craving
prognosis: Nirvana
cure: eightfold path

The gradual meditation on emptiness can be seen to relate to each of these four aspects. Insight into *dukkha/duḥkha* forms an undercurrent throughout the gradual meditation on emptiness, through the relentless emphasis in the instructions on what type of disturbance or weariness has been overcome with each step and what type of disturbance or weariness still remains. In addition, the perceptions of earth and of infinite space offer a substantial contribution to insight into *dukkha/duḥkha*, as they can reveal the affliction caused due to a misunderstanding of the true nature of the material dimension of experience. Much of the pervasive suffering that exists in this world is an outcome of an unwise handling and even outright misunderstanding of the nature of material phenomena.

The pathogen identified in the teaching of the four noble truths is craving. This relates closely to the important role played by the mind in constructing the drama of existence, which can emerge with considerable clarity from sustained engagement with the perception of infinite consciousness as a step in the gradual meditation on emptiness. It is precisely this central role of the mind that underlies the identification of craving as the chief culprit for the arising of *dukkha/duḥkha* in the second noble truth.

The cessation of *dukkha/duḥkha* envisaged in the third noble truth, corresponding to the realization of Nirvana, pivots on the complete eradication of selfing and conceit, on the thorough abandoning of clinging by way of my-making and appropriation. In the gradual meditation on emptiness, in the way presented in the preceding pages, the same topic is central for implementing the perception of nothingness. From this perspective, the third noble truth points to the culmination of such practice, whereby all selfing will be forever abandoned. This then corresponds to the peak of emptiness, the "purified, supreme, and unsurpassed entry into emptiness" reached with the eradication of the influxes.

The noble eightfold path presents the required cure, providing the needed context for actual meditation practice. The directional input of right view informs right intention, which stands in the background of right speech, action, and livelihood as central dimensions of daily life, together with their meditative complements in right effort, right mindfulness, and right concentration.

The practice presented here relies on the overall orientation and the ethical orientation established through the first two of these path factors, right view and right intention, leading to an alignment of the next three factors concerned with conduct, based on which the actual practice of the gradual meditation can be seen as an implementation of the last three path factors in particular. According to a presentation found elsewhere among the early discourses, the five path factors of right view, intention, effort, mindfulness, and concentration are directly relevant to actual meditation practice, whereas the path factors of right speech, action, and livelihood need to have been cultivated previously.[154] In other words, these are the indispensable foundation for any engagement with early Buddhist meditation and therefore also for the gradual entry into emptiness. Ethics and wisdom need each other and stand in a close interrelationship, comparable to two hands that are washing each other.[155] Genuine progress in realization of emptiness requires an ethical foundation and expresses itself in ethical behavior. Early Buddhist thought leaves no room for separating ethics from emptiness, which would be as meaningless as trying to wash our hand just with the fingers of the same hand, rather than relying on our second hand for that purpose.

Based on a firm ethical foundation, mindfulness features as a key quality throughout the gradual meditation on emptiness. Such meditation actualizes the effort of arousing and cultivating what is wholesome, thereby gradually emptying the mind of what is unwholesome. The relevance of concentration is evident in the recurrent reference to the experience of oneness. Achieving and maintaining such meditative oneness requires a high degree of mindfulness in order to remain stable, which for several of these meditative perceptions needs to be achieved in the absence of a circumscribed object that could serve as a support for focusing the mind. Due to the implementation of the other path factors, the concentration cultivated here pertains to the category of being "right," which above all requires contextualization of a path factor with the others.[156] The central orientation of the meditative path of practice in the present case revolves in particular around a deconstruction of experience as a way of leading directly to the final goal of Nirvana. For this reason, the overall orientation clearly falls in the category of being right, due to being aimed at facilitating a realization of the third noble truth.

3. Dependent Arising

The second noble truth highlights a key dimension of the teaching on dependent arising (*paṭicca samuppāda / pratītya samutpāda*), namely the role of craving in leading to various manifestations of *dukkha/duḥkha*. An aspect in the standard presentation of such dependent arising of particular relevance to the instructions in the Smaller Discourse on Emptiness is the reciprocal conditioning between consciousness and name-and-form (see above p. 82). By cultivating the perceptions of earth and of infinite space in the course of the gradual meditation on emptiness, the experience of form comes to be gradually divested of its material foundation, as a result of which the five fingers of name can only lay hold of space. With the perception of infinite consciousness, attention turns back to the knowing part of the mind, rather than becoming involved with the proliferative activities of the other fingers of name. Practice undertaken in this way has a remarkable potential to undermine craving and clinging and thereby to lead to freedom from *dukkha/duḥkha*.

In addition to its potential in offering a practical way to explore the reciprocal conditioning between consciousness and name-and-form, the gradual meditation on emptiness is also relevant to the two factors that, in the standard description of dependent arising by way of twelve links, precede consciousness. These are volitional activities and ignorance. As long as ignorance exerts its deluding influence, volitional activities will operate under the illusory notion of a self, be it as the fully fledged belief in the existence of such a self or else just in the form of the remnants of such a belief in the form of conceit and appropriation. In a way, selfing is the key operator behind all distractions and ruminations, whose aimless ambling around often seems to serve mainly the purpose of propping up the fragile sense of there being a self. With the perception of nothingness, this sense of self comes to be deconstructed, thereby gradually reducing volitional activities under the influence of the ignorant tendency toward selfing.

Ignorance itself can then become the target of signless concentration, in particular if such practice is undertaken within the context of the gradual meditation on emptiness. Now, it is indeed the case that this type of concentration results in a reduced level of mental functioning that makes it no longer possible to cultivate insight. However, cultivating signlessness can have a rather profound impact on how we subsequently view ordinary mental activity, as it can lead to an increasingly better understanding of the construction of experiences. This is precisely what gradually erodes ignorance.

In sum, the trajectory of the gradual meditation on emptiness in leading to liberation can be seen to relate specifically to the first four links of dependent arising: ignorance, volitional activities, consciousness, and name-and-form. This relationship sets out by deconstructing form, then substantially diminishes the impact of name, divests volitional activities of their supposed epicenter in a self, and reveals the operational mechanism of ignorance evident in the constructed nature of experience.

4. Conditionality in Meditation

In addition to the above, the topic of conditionality as such forms a continuous undercurrent in the instructions for abiding in emptiness. This takes the form of introducing each step with the indication that its unitary experience is something *dependent* on the relevant perception. In the case of infinite consciousness, for example, one "attends to oneness *in dependence on* the perception of the sphere of infinite consciousness." In this way, there is an explicit marker of conditionality built into the description of the experience of oneness. The providing of such markers continues with the instructions on disturbances. Staying with the same example, once the oneness *in dependence on* the perception of the sphere of infinite consciousness has been successfully cultivated, disturbances that may occur *in dependence on* the perceptions of earth and infinite space are no longer present. Yet, what is still present is nevertheless a remainder of disturbance, namely precisely the "oneness *in dependence on* the perception of the sphere of infinite consciousness." The marker of conditionality comes up again with the clarification that the oneness *in dependence on* the present perception corresponds to the non-emptiness that is still left.

The undercurrent of inculcating awareness of conditionality established in this way serves to drive home again and again that each meditative experience of emptiness is still within the realm of what is conditioned. However profound a particular experience of oneness may appear to be from the subjective viewpoint, it is nevertheless merely a product of conditions. Such recurrent highlighting of conditionality can be understood to complement the repeated pointers provided by considering each meditative step as corresponding to a remainder of disturbance or weariness. A challenge of this particular approach to liberation is, as already mentioned earlier, that some of these perceptual experiences can become quite exhilarating and therefore can give rise to conceit and appropriation. This tendency can be countered with the help of maintaining a continuous, clear awareness that even this is still conditioned; it is just a product of having cultivated the appropriate conditions in the course of our meditation practice.

5. The Unconditioned

Continuous awareness of the conditionality of each step in the gradual meditation on emptiness prepares the ground for the understanding to be aroused at the present juncture, namely that "this signless concentration of the mind is also conditioned and produced by volition." Despite its sublime and profound nature, being beyond fabrication and mental construction, still, even signlessness is something that has been produced by volition; it, too, is conditioned. Admittedly, this is not necessarily self-evident, precisely due to its characteristic of stepping out of the usual conditionality of constructing experience by letting go of all signs. As mentioned earlier (see above p. 117), the term *nimitta*, "sign," carries a causal nuance. Hence, the absence of any *nimitta* can give the mistaken impression that we have already gone beyond conditionality. Yet, although Nirvana is of course signless and the meditative experience of signlessness comes as close as possible to the experience of Nirvana, signless concentration as such is not a level of awakening, and its experience does not imply a realization of Nirvana.[157]

Since the experience of signlessness is beyond concepts, an understanding of its conditionality needs to be to some extent retrospective, as it requires taking up signs at least briefly in order to be able to have the concepts of "conditioned" and "produced by volition." With the proper preparation laid through having attended to conditionality with each of the preceding steps, it becomes easier to see through the present step as well and discern its conditioned nature. Due to having trained ourselves in seeing conditionality, the amount of effort required to arouse such understanding diminishes, simply because increasing familiarity facilitates the activation of this insight. In this way, familiarity with conditionality as an intrinsic feature of the meditative perceptions enables stepping out of signlessness just for a fraction of a moment to arouse the needed understanding and be able to return swiftly to abiding in signlessness, accompanied by the non-attachment born of insight.

This then leads to the complementary understanding that "whatever is conditioned and produced by volition, that is impermanent and of a nature to cease." The experience of oneness in dependence on signless concentration of the mind does not naturally call up the quality of impermanence, simply because its nature—at least once we have developed sufficient familiarity with this meditative step to be able to abide in it for longer periods without distraction—is so still and peaceful. Yet, what is conditioned must be impermanent. Moreover, the qualification in the instruction that signless concentration is of a nature to cease can be taken to point to a key aspect for enabling the breakthrough to Nirvana. This can occur when the present moment ceases and the next moment has not yet arisen. The breakthrough to awakening can be understood to be "located," if this term can be used at all, at the outer edge of the ending of the present moment if, and only if, we do not reach out for or lean into the next moment. A helpful indication in a Pāli discourse provides the following instruction:[158]

> For one who is not intending and not volitionally constructing, those very perceptions cease, other coarse perceptions do not arise, and one experiences cessation.

6. The Awakening Factors

Besides requiring a relinquishment of everything, by allowing present perceptions to cease without arousing others, another important condition for the breakthrough to awakening to take place is the presence of the seven awakening factors in the mind: mindfulness, investigation-of-phenomena, energy, joy, tranquility, concentration, and equipoise.[159] The sequence of their listing reflects their step-by-step arousal, in that, based on having established mindfulness, we investigate, and such investigation is sustained by energy and results in joy. Out of such joy body and mind become tranquil, we become naturally concentrated, and the whole progression culminates in equipoise.

The awakening factors being aroused, the key for their continuous cultivation is to abide in a mind that is enriched by the presence of these seven and to keep them in balance. Based on the foundation laid by mindfulness, the factors of investigation-of-phenomena, energy, and joy can arouse the mind when this is needed, whereas tranquility, concentration, and equipoise can calm the mind whenever this is opportune.

The balanced presence of the awakening factors can ripen into awakening on being combined with four insight themes, which are seclusion, dispassion, cessation, and letting go. The first of these, seclusion, is a topic already broached at the outset of the gradual meditation on emptiness through the perception of the forest, which continues throughout the whole trajectory. The perceptions of earth and infinite space have a considerable potential in fostering dispassion, in particular toward material things, which with the ensuing perceptions comes to include the mental side of experience as well. The perceptions of infinite consciousness and nothingness in turn leave behind objects and then the subject itself, which can be related to cessation, a topic that continues to be relevant for the final part of the meditative progression. With signlessness and Nirvana, the theme of letting go, which has been another continuous undercurrent of the whole series of perceptions, becomes particularly prominent and comprehensive.[160] Understood in this way, the trajectory of the gradual meditation on emptiness can cover these four insight themes, ripening each of these in the course of the previously cultivated practice and insight, with the letting go into the realization of Nirvana being their final culmination.

It is perhaps from this perspective that the awakening potential of cultivating signless concentration can best be understood. Since such a mode of meditation trains the mind in letting go of all signs, it prepares us for the most thorough letting go required for the breakthrough to awakening. Moreover, selfing is at its weakest at this point. Already the previous step of nothingness has thoroughly undermined any tendency to hold on to a sense of self. The absence of all signs achieved with the next step then corresponds to the absence of all those props usually employed to construe a sense of self, thereby clearing out all possibility of somehow, in some way, reverting to selfing. In combination, the perceptions of nothingness and signlessness make letting go completely of all self-referentiality particularly easy. From this perspective, the progression from nothingness to signlessness could even be considered a form of rehearsal, in the sense that it offers a training in the ability to let go, in particular to let go of a sense of self, which is so crucial for the realization of Nirvana. The basic principle for enabling such a breakthrough could perhaps be captured with the following verse, being a statement reportedly made by the Buddha:[161]

> Apart from letting go of everything,
> I see no safety for sentient beings.

The need to let go, in order to find safety, could be complemented with another verse, which proceeds as follows:[162]

> Having nothing, taking up nothing:
> This is the unsurpassable island.
> I call it "Nirvana,"
> The destruction of old age and death.

7. Summary

The gradual meditation on emptiness comes to its completion with the supreme emptiness reached once the mind has been voided of defilements. This is the peak of walking in the footsteps of the Buddha, to the extent to which this is possible for someone living as his disciple, namely the complete eradication of the three influxes of sensuality, becoming, and ignorance.

The same form of practice can be seen as an implementation of the scheme of the four noble truths. The perceptions of earth and infinite space can deepen our appreciation of *dukkha/duḥkha*, the experience of infinite consciousness highlights the crucial role of the mind and thus corresponds to the centrality of the role of craving, nothingness as the absence of self naturally relates to Nirvana, and the series of emptiness perceptions takes place within the framework of the eightfold path and actualizes its meditative dimension.

Another perspective on the gradual meditation on emptiness can rely on the first four links of the twelvefold presentation of dependent arising. The perceptions of earth and infinite space reduce and then leave behind materiality, whereby name-and-form in a way reduces to name. With infinite consciousness the activity of name becomes reduced to just attending to the knowing part of the mind, thereby holding name in check. Insight into not self, which with the perception of nothingness substantially reduces ignorant volitional activities, has its complement in signlessness as a way of revealing the construction of experience, thereby significantly reducing ignorance. In this way, the ground is well prepared for the complete cessation of dependent arising with the realization of Nirvana.

The topic of conditionality forms an undercurrent of the practice instructions, which keep highlighting that the oneness experienced *depends* on the particular perception cultivated, which at the same time is the disturbance and non-emptiness still present at this stage. The continuous awareness of conditionality inculcated in this way through the series of increasingly subtle and refined perceptions prepares the ground for the breakthrough to the unconditioned.

This breakthrough requires the insight that "this signless concentration of the mind is also conditioned and produced by volition." Brief moments of taking up signs just enough to arouse this insight can alternate with longer periods of just abiding in signlessness, informed by the inner attitude resulting from this insight. This can lead on to the understanding that "whatever is conditioned and produced by volition, that is impermanent and of a nature to cease." Arousing such understanding calls for an awareness of the process character of all mental experiences, including that of signlessness, with an emphasis on the ending of the present moment.

Ripening the condition of the mind for the breakthrough to awakening requires cultivating the seven awakening factors: mindfulness, investigation-of-phenomena, energy, joy, tranquility, concentration, and equipoise. These need to be balanced with each other and related to the themes of seclusion, dispassion, cessation, and letting go. Closer inspection shows that these four insight themes come up in one way or another during the previous steps of the gradual meditation on emptiness. Proceeding further then calls in particular for a thorough and comprehensive letting go.

8. Practical Instructions

Whether the gradual meditation on emptiness is undertaken for the purpose of realizing Nirvana depends of course on the aspiration of the individual practitioner. Up to the present juncture, the whole trajectory from perception of the forest to signlessness can equally well be of benefit for those whose aspiration is not to gain such realization as soon as possible, be this because Nirvana appears too radical and unappealing a solution to the human predicament or because of wanting to allow for the time needed to perfect the qualities required for becoming a Buddha in the future. Those who do wish to gain stream-entry and higher levels of awakening, however, may decide to opt for combining a progression through the preceding steps with a cultivation of the awakening factors and a clear noting of the dimension of conditionality underlying this progression in order to facilitate the breakthrough to awakening.

This breakthrough can in principle occur at any time during the gradual meditation on emptiness, as long as the inner aspiration for the realization of Nirvana is firmly in place, resulting in the willingness and ability to let go completely. Nevertheless, the final step in the meditative trajectory is particularly apt for facilitating such a breakthrough.

An emphasis on noting conditionality during the progression of the gradual meditation on emptiness revolves around the disturbances or forms of weariness left behind with each step. This begins with leaving behind conditions for disturbances of a physical or mental type through the seclusion afforded by the perception of the forest. The condition for the disturbances created by dualistic contrasts and by the alienation and fragmentation that result from excessive individualism can be left behind with the perception of earth. Next comes the condition for a large range of physical and mental afflictions due to attachment to manifestations of matter, which is left behind through the perception of infinite space. Then the basic condition for the bifurcation of experience through the creation of the subject-object duality can be left behind with the perception of infinite consciousness. Next, the key condition for defilements is to be left behind: selfing. This leads on to leaving behind the basic conditions for the construction of experience through signlessness. Noting the gradual reduction of conditionality and its palpable repercussions in increasingly peaceful modes of abiding can prepare the mind for letting go into the supreme peace of the unconditioned.

The cultivation of the awakening factors takes off from the foundation laid by *mindfulness*, which is perhaps the most important mental quality for the entire meditative trajectory. Based on mindfulness being established, an attitude of interest, *investigation*, and even curiosity can enliven the practice. In relation to the individual perceptions, this can take the form of scrutinizing if the present experience is indeed free of the disturbances that should have been left behind at this juncture. Such scrutinizing is not a matter of sustained conceptual engagement but more one of having a close look at the present condition of the mind: Are the hindrances indeed absent, at least temporarily? Is the sameness of earth indeed being clearly seen? Has matter truly been left behind in subjective experience? Is there indeed no other object but the mind itself? Has selfing gone fully into abeyance?

The same type of query could in principle also be related to signlessness, in the sense of investigating if all signs have indeed been left behind. The problem, however, is that undertaking such inquiry would involve taking up signs. For this reason, it seems best to relate the intentional arousal of the awakening factors mainly to the preceding steps. Based on their sustained cultivation throughout the previous meditative trajectory, with the experience of signlessness we in a way continue to surf on the momentum already established, without needing any further effort—in particular without needing to reach out for signs—in order for the presence of the awakening factors to continue. Such continuity manifests mainly in mindful equipoise imbued with the subtle joy of contentment. These can accompany the experience of signlessness together with an element of what could perhaps best be called a subtle form of curiosity. If it were to be expressed conceptually, such curiosity would take the form of inquiring if all signs have indeed been left behind, if there is even a trace of reaching out for any sign. Since the present stage is non-conceptual, however, what the presence of such curiosity amounts to is mainly a silent and watchful attitude of interest. The presence of this attitude ensures that the abiding in signlessness continues to be fresh and lively, rather than becoming stale and stagnant.

The challenge here is simply that the mind can go into autopilot mode even with signlessness. This would be a dead end. In other words, the idea is not to encourage fixating on a particular experience of absence and then reproduce that again and again, but to adopt a flexible and dynamic attitude of letting go of any fixation. The resultant experience of signlessness is therefore never exactly the same. This subtle element of novelty present in every moment of abiding in signlessness is precisely what "curiosity" can discover. Through the presence of such curiosity as a non-conceptual and effortless continuity of the awakening factor of investigation, any going into autopilot mode can be avoided and the experience of signlessness can unfold its full transformative potential.

Such a modality of practice can at times also be opportune for the previous steps, namely at a time when the mind inclines more to calm abiding, and the complexity of calling up the awakening factors appears almost like an additional disturbance or weariness. In such a case, it can be preferable to arouse them once at the outset, even just briefly, and then simply continue abiding in their presence without calling them up individually with each perception. At other times, however, arousing them deliberately can enliven our meditation.

Whether it be just once at the outset or repeatedly with each perception, based on having investigated the present perception in the manner described above, the next step is to sustain the resultant condition. For each of the perceptions under discussion here, this is respectively the absence of the hindrances, sameness, matter being left behind, objects being relinquished, and selfing gone into abeyance. Such sustaining calls for *energy*, which facilitates maintaining the respective condition of the mind without slackening. The application of energy here is not at all something pushy or forceful, but much rather a soft and gentle type of continuity. Whether it has been possible to achieve such continuity without becoming pushy can be seen reflected in the ease and naturalness with which *joy* arises. If there is too much pushiness, joy will not manifest. Additional sources for the arousal of joy are awareness of the disturbances left behind and the mind being well established in the present moment.

The absence of the respective disturbances and the presence of those awakening factors that have already been aroused result in a sense of *tranquility* that pervades body and mind. In this tranquil condition, it becomes much easier to remain concentrated on the particular perception that has been taken up, without succumbing to distraction. As mentioned repeatedly, such *concentration* is not a matter of focusing. Instead, the cultivation of concentration here much rather takes the form of an inclusive composure of the mind. All of this then culminates in a superb degree of mental *equipoise*, grounded in the different dimensions of emptiness that each of the steps in the gradual meditative trajectory has revealed.

The awakening factors being established, there is a need to balance them. If the mind becomes slightly sluggish while abiding in any of the perceptions under discussion, then a bit more emphasis can be given to interest (investigation/curiosity) as a means of rousing energy and experiencing joy. If instead the mind becomes slightly agitated, even just becoming a bit overenergized, slightly more importance can be given to relaxing into the present perception and experiencing the tranquility of having left behind the respective disturbances, as a means for the mind to become collected and equipoised. Once such balance of the awakening factors has been well established during the first five perceptions, it can continue effortlessly through the sixth perception of signlessness, which by dint of dropping all signs would no longer be amenable to an intentional cultivation or even an intentional balancing of the awakening factors.

With the awakening factors established and balanced, the usual pattern for actualizing their awakening potential requires being based on seclusion, dispassion, and cessation, inclining toward letting go. In the course of the previous trajectory of the gradual meditation on emptiness, however, all of these insight themes have already been established. For this reason, at the stage of signlessness it becomes possible to proceed without needing to take up signs, which would be required for calling up each of these insight themes individually. In other words, just as the awakening factors are present due to having been cultivated with the previous steps, in the same way seclusion, dispassion, cessation, and letting go are already present, at least to some degree. Through having given attention to conditionality in the way described above, the conditioned nature of signlessness also becomes apparent without needing much deliberation. It follows that at the present juncture an inclining toward Nirvana requires mainly a sense of the experience of signlessness as a process, which corresponds to insight into its impermanence, and an awareness directed in particular to the ending aspect of every moment of this process.

Although at first even such practice will require some minimal taking up of signs, with more familiarity this can be diminished sufficiently to enable a continuous abiding in signlessness. The perception of the present moment's experience as a process can be compared to sitting in a train, where alongside various experiences there is a sense of moving forward. This sense of being in motion usually is very much at the background of attention and does not interfere with the ability to have a conversation, read, etc. A similar sense of being in motion can be cultivated throughout any type of activity as a reflection of impermanence. Walking meditation is particularly apt for getting started on this way of viewing experience.

Once such awareness of the process character of experience has become sufficiently familiar, there can be more emphasis on the ending of every moment rather than on its arising. This is not a matter of resorting to momentariness; it does not imply that everything ceases completely in every single moment. The point is only to highlight that everything passes away sooner or later, that everything is bound to vanish eventually. If this type of perspective has been cultivated in daily life or with other forms of meditation, it can more easily be related to the experience of signlessness. The breakthrough to Nirvana can happen when it becomes possible to allow the present moment to cease without mentally reaching out for the next moment. This is in a way the supreme letting go, a culmination of the training in progressive levels of letting go that have been cultivated throughout the gradual meditation on emptiness.

As a way of conveying the culmination point of the gradual meditation on emptiness, central qualities of the mind that result from such abiding could be summarized under the acronym "CEASE," based on the first letter of each of the following five qualities:

Clear
Empty
Awake
Silent
Equanimous

Based on pursuing the meditative trajectory up to signlessness, the mind has become increasingly *clear*, comparable to a cloudless sky. Some practice traditions refer to this aspect instead as a form of luminosity of the mind, but I find the notion of clarity preferable here. The presence of such clarity combines with the complete absence of any I-making and my-making, the mind being thoroughly *empty* of any self-referentiality. At the same time, it is fully *awake* in the sense of alertness to the present moment with a sense of freshness. In the absence of conceptual proliferations, the mind has become very *silent*, naturally unified without any fixation. All of this combines in a state of profound balance due to the absence of even a trace of wanting or rejecting, whereby the mind has become superbly *equanimous*. At this point, the five qualities Clear, Empty, Awake, Still, and Equanimous can converge on allowing everything to CEASE, in the sense of a complete letting go without holding on to anything at all.

In order to prepare for such a complete letting go, it can be helpful to cultivate insightful reflections related to signlessness during times of not actually practicing it, particularly when just emerging from it. This can take the form of arousing the clear understanding that even this sublime meditative experience, so free from mental activity of any kind, is still something conditioned, however subtle it may be. It is still a product of intentions and for this reason should neither be delighted in nor be turned into something that we appropriate. The constructed nature of even this experience implies that it is also impermanent and bound to cease. Hence, better not attach to it.

The power of the letting go that is possible through the above reflections, in whatever way this can best be adjusted to our personal needs and preferences, relies on the degree to which previous practice has brought home the fact of disturbance or weariness in relation to each step in the gradual meditation on emptiness. This corresponds to insight into *dukkha/duḥkha* and thereby performs a crucial function for bringing the present meditative trajectory to its successful completion. Insight into disturbance or weariness can benefit considerably from proceeding through the progression of perceptions backward. Moving from signlessness, via nothingness, infinite consciousness, infinite space, and earth, to the perception of the forest, a notable increase in disturbance and weariness manifests. The resultant deepening understanding of *dukkha/duḥkha* can empower proceeding forward again through the series of perceptions leading to signlessness and perhaps, when the time is ripe, even further.

For completing the full trajectory of emptiness, the mind needs to be voided of defilements. This is supreme emptiness indeed. The personal transformation that results from the eradication of defilements is the true measuring rod for successful contemplation of emptiness. The whole practice described in this book is not about creating extraordinary meditative experiences, although these are indeed part of the path of practice, but about opening the heart and releasing it from the grip of defilements so that it can flower into the beauty of the divine abodes in any daily-life situation.

The meditation session can conclude with the usual sharing of merits, which at this point can become particularly powerful due to the profundity of the meditation. Practice in daily life simply requires keeping the mind as empty as possible of defilements. This corresponds to the instructions taken up in the first chapter (see above p. 5). While abiding by way of this abiding in emptiness, we learn to maintain the absence of defilements when being in any of the four postures, when talking, and even when thinking. This is the key to genuine continuity in abiding in emptiness.

With this final correspondence established, the whole of the meditative trajectory presented here can be seen to combine a linear progression with a circular dimension. The linear progression leads from building a foundation in letting go of defilements during any activities to advancing step by step through the perceptions of the forest, earth, infinite space, infinite consciousness, nothingness, signlessness, and Nirvana. The circular dimension underlying this linear progression has its turning point in the transition from infinite space to infinite consciousness. In a way, these are simply two complementary perspectives on the same experience, as the knowing of infinite space, by dint of the object taken, has become infinite itself. The next step of nothingness then complements the perception of earth in regard to insight into the absence of a self; signlessness complements the perception of the forest in matters of absence in general; and Nirvana complements daily-life practice on the all-important topic ofbeing empty of defilements. In this way, a circle results that leads from daily life to the breakthrough to Nirvana, whose realization in turn directly feeds back into daily life, since the most crucial repercussions of a full realization of emptiness manifest in remaining balanced and at ease, free from any defiled reactions, even in the most challenging circumstances of daily life.

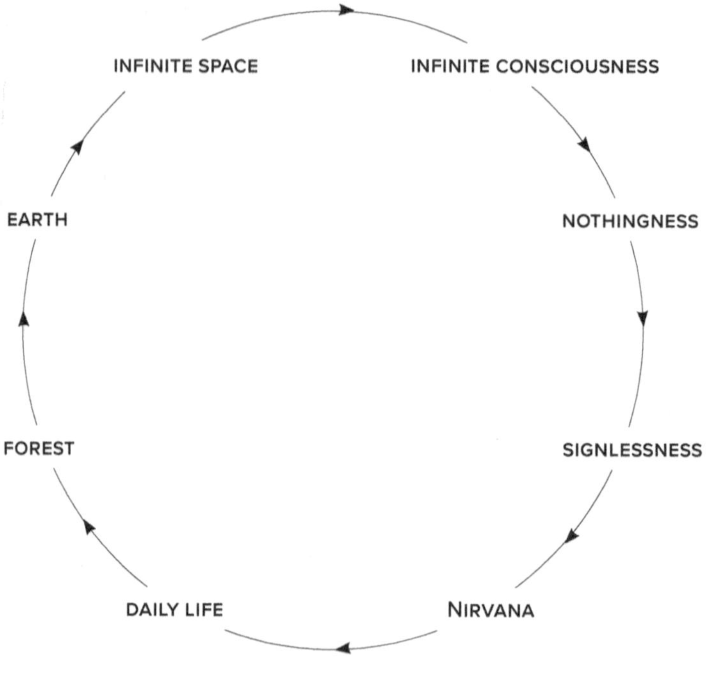

Abbreviations

Abhidh-k	*Abhidharmakośabhāṣya*
AN	*Aṅguttaranikāya*
B^{e}	Burmese edition
CBETA	Chinese Buddhist Electronic Text Association
C^{e}	Ceylonese edition
D	Derge edition
DĀ	*Dīrghāgama* (T 1)
Dhp	*Dhammapada*
DN	*Dīghanikāya*
EĀ	*Ekottarikāgama* (T 125)
E^{e}	Pali Text Society edition
MĀ	*Madhyamāgama* (T 26)
MN	*Majjhimanikāya*
P	Peking edition
Ps	*Papañcasūdanī*
SĀ	*Saṃyuktāgama* (T 99)
SĀ^{2}	*Saṃyuktāgama* (T 100)
S^{e}	Siamese edition
SHT	Sanskrithandschriften aus den Turfanfunden
SN	*Saṃyuttanikāya*
Sn	*Suttanipāta*

T	Taishō edition (CBETA)
Th	*Theragāthā*
Ud	*Udāna*
Up	*Abhidharmakośopāyikāṭīkā*
Vin	*Vinaya*
Vism	*Visuddhimagga*

Notes

1. On the notion of "early Buddhism" see also Anālayo 2023a.
2. Anālayo 2015.
3. Anālayo 2023b.
4. On this challenge see Treleaven 2018.
5. See below note 27.
6. MN 122 at MN III 112,31: *tassa ce, ānanda, bhikkhuno iminā vihārena viharato caṅkamāya cittaṃ namati, so caṅkamati: evaṃ maṃ caṅkamantaṃ nābhijjhādomanassā pāpakā akusalā dhammā anvāssavissantī ti; itiha tattha sampajāno hoti.* Here and elsewhere, I employ plural in English where the Pāli original has the singular, as part of an attempt to present the instructions in a gender-inclusive way.
7. Unfortunately, the practical implications of the preceding part in the discourse are difficult to ascertain. Although the relevant part beginning in MN 122 at MN III 111,6 (translated by Ñāṇamoli 1995/2005, 972) has parallels in Chinese and Tibetan, which could in principle help to provide a clarifying perspective on the meditative abiding in emptiness internally and externally, the complex situation resulting from a comparison of the parallels does not, at least as far as I am able to see, point to a solution; see Anālayo 2011a, 690–94. This prevents me from presenting a form of formal meditation based on MN 122.
8. Plofker 2009, 16 and 56.
9. MĀ 191 at T 1.26.739a13 (translated by Anālayo 2012a, 48 or 2015, 116) and Skilling 1994, 220,15.
10. MN 122 at MN III 113,1: *tassa ce, ānanda, bhikkhuno iminā vihārena viharato ṭhānāya cittaṃ namati, so tiṭṭhati: evaṃ maṃ ṭhitaṃ* (C^e and E^e: *tiṭṭhantaṃ*) *nābhijjhādomanassā pāpakā akusalā dhammā anvāssavissantī ti; itiha tattha sampajāno hoti. tassa ce, ānanda, bhikkhuno iminā vihārena viharato nisajjāya cittaṃ namati, so nisīdati: evaṃ maṃ nisinnaṃ nābhijjhādomanassā pāpakā akusalā dhammā anvāssavissantī ti; itiha tattha sampajāno hoti. tassa ce, ānanda, bhikkhuno iminā vihārena viharato sayanāya cittaṃ namati, so sayati: evaṃ maṃ sayantaṃ nābhijjhādomanassā pāpakā akusalā dhammā anvāssavissantī ti; itiha tattha sampajāno hoti.*
11. MN 10 at MN I 57,2 (translated by Ñāṇamoli 1995/2005, 146). The four postures occur also in one of the two Chinese *Āgama* parallels, which additionally mentions the occasions of falling asleep and waking up; see MĀ 98 at T 1.26.582b21 (translated by Anālayo 2013b, 270).
12. See, e.g., SN 47.13 at SN V 163,14 (translated by Bodhi 2000, 1644) and its parallel

SĀ 638 at T 2.99.177a10 (translated by Anālayo 2016b, 122). The two parallels agree in recommending such practice as a way of becoming self-reliant.

13. SN 22.100 at SN III 151,6 (translated by Bodhi 2000, 958), with a parallel in SĀ 267 at T 2.99.69c5 (translated by Anālayo 2013a, 43), which does not mention all four postures.

14. MN 122 at MN III 113,12: *tassa ce, ānanda, bhikkhuno iminā vihārena viharato kathāya* (E^e^ and S^e^: *bhāsāya*) *cittaṃ namati, so yāyaṃ kathā hīnā gammā pothujjanikā anariyā anatthasaṃhitā* (S^e^: *anatthasañhitā*) *na nibbidāya na virāgāya na nirodhāya na upasamāya na abhiññāya na sambodhāya na nibbānāya saṃvattati, seyyathīdaṃ* (B^e^: *seyyathidaṃ*) *rājakathā corakathā mahāmattakathā senākathā bhayakathā yuddhakathā annakathā pānakathā vatthakathā sayanakathā mālākathā gandhakathā ñātikathā yānakathā gāmakathā nigamakathā nagarakathā janapadakathā itthikathā* (C^e^ adds *purisakathā*) *sūrakathā* (B^e^ and C^e^: *surākathā*) *visikhākathā kumbhaṭṭhānakathā pubbapetakathā nānattakathā lokakkhāyikā samuddakkhāyikā itibhavābhavakathā iti vā iti* (S^e^: without *iti*), *evarūpiṃ* (S^e^: *evarūpaṃ*) *kathaṃ na kathessāmī ti; itiha tattha sampajāno hoti. yā ca kho* (S^e^: without *kho*) *ayaṃ, ānanda, kathā abhisallekhikā cetovinīvaraṇasappāyā* (E^e^: *cetovivaraṇasappāyā*; S^e^: *cetovicāraṇasappāyā*) *ekantanibbidāya virāgāya nirodhāya upasamāya abhiññāya sambodhāya nibbānāya saṃvattati, seyyathīdaṃ* (B^e^: *seyyathidaṃ*) *appicchakathā santuṭṭhikathā pavivekakathā asaṃsaggakathā viriyārambhakathā* (B^e^: *vīriyārambhakathā*) *sīlakathā samādhikathā paññākathā vimuttikathā vimuttiñāṇadassanakathā iti, evarūpiṃ kathaṃ kathessāmī ti; itiha tattha sampajāno hoti.* Adopting the variant *cetovinīvaraṇasappāyā* would receive support from the parallels MĀ 191 at T 1.739b1: 無諸陰蓋 (translated by Anālayo 2012a, 49 or 2015, 187) and Skilling 1994, 230,1: *sems kyi sgrib pa med pa*; see also a similar listing of suitable conversations in an otherwise unrelated passage in the *Śrāvakabhūmi*, Śrāvakabhūmi Study Group 1998, 220,12, which introduces commendable talk as *cetovinivaraṇasāṃpreyagāminīṃ*.

15. See also Anālayo 2022d, 14 for a more detailed division of the list.

16. MN 13 at MN I 86,28 (translated by Ñāṇamoli 1995/2005, 181), with parallels in MĀ 99 at T 1.26.585a29 (translated by Anālayo and Bucknell 2020, 240), T 1.53.847b2, EĀ 21.9 at T 2.125.605a28, and T 17.737.539c25.

17. MN 5 at MN I 32,26 (translated by Ñāṇamoli 1995/2005, 114), with parallels in MĀ 87 at T 1.26.569c5 (translated by Anālayo and Bucknell 2020, 166), T 1.49.842a15, and EĀ 25.6 at T 2.125.634a6.

18. MN 122 at MN III 113,32: *tassa ce, ānanda, bhikkhuno iminā vihārena viharato vitakkāya cittaṃ namati, so ye te* (E^e^ and S^e^: *me*) *vitakkā hīnā gammā pothujjanikā anariyā anatthasaṃhitā* (S^e^: *anatthasañhitā*) *na nibbidāya na virāgāya na nirodhāya na upasamāya na abhiññāya na sambodhāya na nibbānāya saṃvattanti, seyyathīdaṃ* (B^e^: *seyyathidaṃ*) *kāmavitakko byāpādavitakko* (C^e^: *vyāpādavitakko*) *vihiṃsāvitakko iti evarūpe vitakke na vitakkessāmī ti; itiha tattha sampajāno hoti. ye ca kho ime* (S^e^ without *ime*), *ānanda, vitakkā ariyā niyyānikā niyyanti takkarassa sammādukkhakkhayāya, seyyathīdaṃ* (B^e^: *seyyathidaṃ*) *nekkhammavitakko abyāpādavitakko* (C^e^: *avyāpādavitakko*) *avihiṃsāvitakko iti evarūpe vitakke vitakkessāmī ti; itiha tattha sampajāno hoti.*

19. On different modalities of right view see Anālayo 2018a, 30–31.

20. See in more detail Anālayo 2011c.

21. See in more detail Anālayo 2022c, 117–72 and 2022g.
22. DN 33 at DN III 280,27 (translated by Walshe 1987, 500) and its parallels Stache-Rosen 1968, 165, DĀ 9 at T 1.1.52a9, and T 1.12.232a21.
23. See in more detail Anālayo 2017b.
24. MN 19 at MN I 115,21 (translated by Ñāṇamoli 1995/2005, 208), with a parallel in MĀ 102 at T 1.26.589b5; see also the *Śikṣāsamuccaya*, Bendall 1902/1970, 53,19 (translated by Bendall and Rouse 1922/1990, 54) and the *Saundarananda* 15.18, Johnston 1928, 105,1 (translated by Johnston 1932, 83).
25. See in more detail Anālayo 2022c, 211–30.
26. See Anālayo 2015, 151–62.
27. Sn 1119: *suññato lokaṃ avekkhassu ... sadā sato ... evaṃ lokaṃ avekkhantaṃ, maccurājā na passatī ti.*
28. See in more detail Anālayo 2019b, 10.
29. MN 121 at MN III 104,13: *pubbe cāhaṃ* (B^e and C^e: *pubbepāhaṃ*), *ānanda, etarahi ca* (B^e and C^e: *pi*) *suññatāvihārena bahulaṃ viharāmi. seyyathā pi, ānanda, ayaṃ migāramātu pāsādo suñño hatthigavāssavaḷavena* (B^e: *hatthigavassavaḷavena*, S^e: *hatthigavāssavalavena*), *suñño jātarūparajatena, suñño itthipurisasannipātena* (S^e: *itthīpurisasannipātena*) *atthi c' ev' idaṃ asuññataṃ yadidaṃ bhikkhusaṅghaṃ* (E^e: *bhikkhusaṃghaṃ*) *paṭicca ekattaṃ. evam eva kho, ānanda, bhikkhu amanasikaritvā gāmasaññaṃ, amanasikaritvā manussasaññaṃ, araññasaññaṃ paṭicca manasikaroti ekattaṃ. tassa araññasaññāya cittaṃ pakkhandati pasīdati santiṭṭhati adhimuccati* (E^e: *vimuccati*; see also Schmithausen 1981, 234n124). *so evaṃ pajānāti: ye assu darathā gāmasaññaṃ paṭicca te 'dha na santi, ye assu darathā manussasaññaṃ paṭicca te 'dha na santi, atthi c' evāyaṃ darathamattā yadidaṃ araññasaññaṃ paṭicca ekattan ti. so suññam idaṃ saññāgataṃ gāmasaññāyā ti pajānāti, suññam idaṃ saññāgataṃ manussasaññāyā ti pajānāti, atthi c' ev' idaṃ asuññataṃ yadidaṃ araññasaññaṃ paṭicca ekattan ti. iti yaṃ hi kho tattha na hoti, tena taṃ suññaṃ samanupassati, yaṃ pana tattha avasiṭṭhaṃ hoti taṃ santam* (E^e and S^e: *santaṃ*) *idam* (B^e and C^e: *idaṃ*) *atthī ti pajānāti. evam pi 'ssa esā, ānanda, yathābhuccā avipallatthā parisuddhā suññatāvakkanti bhavati.*
30. See Anālayo 2022b, 188.
31. MĀ 190 at T 1.26.737a9 (translated by Anālayo 2012a, 27 or 2015, 177) and Skilling 1994, 150,11; see also Anālayo 2011a, 685.
32. On the notion of the forest as wilderness see also Visigalli 2019.
33. AN 6.42 at AN III 343,9 (translated by Bodhi 2012, 906) and AN 8.86 at AN IV 344,6 (translated by Bodhi 2012, 1235), with a parallel in SĀ 1251 at T 2.99.344a15.
34. MN 4 at MN I 17,6 (translated by Ñāṇamoli 1995/2005, 102) and its parallel EĀ 31.1 at T 2.125.665b22 (translated by Anālayo 2011b, 209).
35. See Anālayo 2019b, 6f.
36. See Gethin 1997.
37. See Anālayo 2016a, 12 and 16.
38. See in more detail Anālayo 2003b, 182–200, 2013b, 177–94, 2018b, 151–69, and 2022e.
39. Magee 2019, 329 offers the following advice: "Calmly, clearly, and with love, we do what we can. And then we let go and let be."
40. MN 145 at MN III 268,14 (translated by Ñāṇamoli 1995/2005, 1118), also found in SN 35.88 at SN II IV 61,13 (translated by Bodhi 2000, 1168), with parallels in SĀ 311

at T 2.99.89b23 and T 1.108.502c24; for further parallels in other texts see Anālayo 2011a, 828.

41. Anālayo 2011a, 684n5.
42. MĀ 190 at T 1.26.737a15: 疲勞.
43. Anālayo 2023b, 171n129.
44. Chalmers 1927, 215 uses "agitation," based on which he then translates the relevant part of the present instruction as follows: "He is clear that the agitation which would attend ideas of a village, or of people, is absent in this conception, but yet there abides some agitation in the solitude which attends the idea of a forest." Noting that "'trouble,' 'disturbance,' or 'distress' [are] renditions that clearly do not apply to the present scripture," Wayman 1997, 279 proposes "embrasure" instead, resulting in the following rendering of the last part of the present instruction: "There is only this measure of embrasure, the singleness depending upon the idea" of the forest. Rossi 2010, 195 opts for the translation "care," so the relevant part becomes as follows: "The cares, which depended on the perception of the village, do not exist anymore. The cares, which depended on the perception of the human being, do not exist anymore. This is, indeed, the only one consisting of care: depending on the singleness based on the perception of wilderness." None of these interesting attempts has been sufficiently compelling for me to adopt it in my translation.
45. See in more detail Anālayo 2022a.
46. See Anālayo 2013b, 142–45.
47. MN 55 at MN I 369,36 (translated by Ñāṇamoli 1995/2005, 102). This part of MN 55 does not appear to have a counterpart in the Sanskrit fragment parallel version; see Anālayo 2011a, 320.
48. Dhp 99: *ramaṇīyāni araññāni, yattha na ramatī jano; vītarāgā ramissanti, na te kāmagavesino*, with Indic language parallels in the Patna *Dharmapada* 155, Cone 1989, 143, and in the *Udānavarga* 29.17, Bernhard 1965, 375 (translated by Anālayo 2019a, 47).
49. MN 121 at MN III 105,3: *puna ca paraṃ, ānanda, bhikkhu amanasikaritvā manussasaññaṃ, amanasikaritvā araññasaññaṃ, paṭhavīsaññaṃ* (B^{e} throughout *pathavī°*; C^{e} throughout *paṭhavi°*) *paṭicca manasikaroti ekattaṃ. tassa paṭhavīsaññāya cittaṃ pakkhandati pasīdati santiṭṭhati adhimuccati* (E^{e}: *vimuccati*). *seyyathā pi, ānanda, āsabhacammaṃ* (E^{e}: *usabhacammaṃ*) *saṅkusatena* (E^{e}: *saṃkusatena*) *suvihataṃ vigatavalikaṃ* (E^{e}: *vigatavasikaṃ*), *evam eva kho, ānanda, bhikkhu yaṃ imissā paṭhaviyā ukkūlavikkūlaṃ* (S^{e}: *ukkulavikulaṃ*) *nadīviduggaṃ khāṇukaṇṭakaṭṭhānaṃ* (E^{e}: *khāṇukaṇṭakādhāraṃ*; C^{e} and S^{e}: *khāṇukaṇṭakadhānaṃ*) *pabbatavisamaṃ, taṃ sabbaṃ amanasikaritvā paṭhavīsaññaṃ paṭicca manasikaroti ekattaṃ. tassa paṭhavīsaññāya* (S^{e}: *paṭhavīsaññā*) *cittaṃ pakkhandati pasīdati santiṭṭhati adhimuccati* (E^{e}: *vimuccati*). *so evaṃ pajānāti: ye assu darathā manussasaññaṃ paṭicca te 'dha na santi, ye assu darathā araññasaññaṃ paṭicca te 'dha na santi, atthi c' evāyaṃ darathamattā yadidaṃ paṭhavīsaññaṃ paṭicca ekattan ti. so suññam idaṃ saññāgataṃ manussasaññāyā ti pajānāti, suññam idaṃ saññāgataṃ araññasaññāyā ti pajānāti, atthi c' ev' idaṃ asuññataṃ yadidaṃ paṭhavīsaññaṃ paṭicca ekattan ti. iti yaṃ hi kho tattha na hoti, tena taṃ suññaṃ samanupassati, yaṃ* (E^{e}: *yam*) *pana tattha avasiṭṭhaṃ hoti, taṃ santam* (E^{e} and S^{e}: *santaṃ*) *idam* (B^{e} and C^{e}: *idaṃ*) *idaṃ atthī ti pajānāti. evam pi 'ssa esā, ānanda, yathābhuccā avipallatthā parisuddhā suññatāvakkanti bhavati.*

50. Wayman 1997, 280 comments on this step that "one holds onto a 'sign' of earth in ... the mind, without permitting its modification into any particular mode of earth. This is a kind of 'voidness' aiming at the pure earth, devoid of any earthly features."
51. Ps IV 153,19: *paṭhavīsaññaṃ paṭicca manasikaroti ekattan ti kasiṇapaṭhavīsaññaṃ yeva paṭicca sambhūtaṃ ekaṃ saññaṃ manasikaroti.*
52. AN 10.25 at AN V 46,3 (translated by Bodhi 2012 1370). In the context of a listing of the eight *abhibhāyatanas*, the first three colors are illustrated in MN 77 at MN II 13,29 (translated by Ñāṇamoli 1995/2005, 639) with the example of flowers: the blue flax flower (*Linum usitatissimum*), the yellow bayur tree flower (*Pterospermum acerifolium*), and the red hibiscus flower (*Pentapetes phoenicea*); the color white then has the morning star as illustration.
53. DN 16 at DN II 144,17 (translated by Walshe 1987, 265), found similarly also in the Sanskrit fragment parallel, Waldschmidt 1951, 298,7, and in DĀ 2 at T 1.1.25c9.
54. See, e.g., Vism 123,28: *kasiṇaṃ kātabbaṃ* (translated by Ñāṇamoli 1991, 123 as: "he should make a kasina"), in reference to the external device to be used to arouse the perception of earth.
55. Vism 172,9 (translated by Ñāṇamoli 1991, 167).
56. Vism 174,19 (translated by Ñāṇamoli 1991, 169).
57. See in more detail Anālayo 2022c, 59–115.
58. T 29.1559.303b18 (Paramārtha; translated by Pruden 1990, 1278), whereas the Sanskrit version, Abhidh-k 8.36, Pradhan 1967, 458,3, and the other Chinese translation, T 29.1558.151c28 (Xuánzàng), only mention the opinion that the wind element is a tangible object.
59. MĀ 190 at T 1.26.737a23 (translated by Anālayo 2012a, 28 or 2015, 177) and Skilling 1994, 156,10.
60. MN 28 at MN I 185,20 (translated by Ñāṇamoli 1995/2005, 279) and its parallel MĀ 30 at T 1.26.464c7 (translated by Bingenheimer, Anālayo, and Bucknell 2013, 219).
61. AN 6.41 at AN III 341,1 (translated by Bodhi 2012, 904) and its parallels SĀ 494 at T 2.99.128c25 and Up 2020 at D 4094 *ju* 58a7 or P 5595 *tu* 64a4. Vism 364,10 (translated by Ñāṇamoli 1991, 358) explicitly applies this perspective to the anatomical parts of the human body, explaining that each of these parts is made up of a combination of the four elements.
62. DN 22 at DN II 294,17 (translated by Walshe 1987, 338), MN 10 at MN I 57,20 (translated by Ñāṇamoli 1995/2005, 148), MĀ 98 at T 1.26.583b19 (translated by Anālayo 2013b, 275), and EĀ 12.1 at T 2.125.568a26 (translated by Anālayo 2013b, 288); see also the *Śikṣāsamuccaya*, Bendall 1902/1970, 210,4 (translated by Bendall and Rouse 1922/1990, 202).
63. Ps I 272,1 (translated by Soma 1941/1981, 103).
64. MN 112 at MN III 31,23 (translated by Ñāṇamoli 1995/2005, 905) and MĀ 187 at T 1.26.733a2 (translated by Anālayo 2008, 250); both versions take up altogether six elements, adding space and consciousness to the four elements.
65. DN 16 at DN II 107,23 (translated by Walshe 1987, 248), Waldschmidt 1951, 212,25, DĀ 2 at T 1.1.15c29, T 1.5.165a28 (without mentioning space), T 1.6.180c15, and T 1.7.191c23.
66. AN 7.62 at AN IV 100,5 (translated by Bodhi 2012, 1071), Dietz 2007 (Sanskrit fragments), MĀ 8 at T 1.26.428c9, T 1.30.811c24, EĀ 40.1 at T 2.125.736b1 (translated

by Anālayo 2019a, 120), Up 3008 (edited and translated by Dietz 2007), and Up 3094 at D 4094 *ju* 187b3 or P 5595 *tu* 214b1; see also Anālayo 2019a, 120–27.

67. AN 4.170 at AN II 157,4 (translated by Bodhi 2012, 535) and its parallel SĀ 560 at T 2.99.146c24 (translated by Anālayo 2009, 192n56).
68. See in more detail Anālayo 2009.
69. Dhp 81: *selo yathā ekaghano, vātena na samīrati, evaṃ nindāpasaṃsāsu, na samiñjanti* (S^e: *sammiñjanti*) *paṇḍitā*, with Indic language parallels in the Gāndhārī *Dharmapada* 239, Brough 1962/2001, 157, the Patna *Dharmapada* 93, Cone 1989, 128, and the *Udānavarga* 29.49, Bernhard 1965, 387; the same image occurs also in a verse in the Mūlasarvāstivāda *Vinaya*, Gnoli 1978, 147,1.
70. On the probable origin of the body scan technique see Anālayo 2020b.
71. MN 121 at MN III 105,25: *puna ca paraṃ, ānanda, bhikkhu amanasikaritvā araññasaññaṃ, amanasikaritvā paṭhavīsaññaṃ* (B^e throughout *pathavī°*; C^e throughout *paṭhavi°*), *ākāsānañcāyatanasaññaṃ paṭicca manasikaroti ekattaṃ. tassa ākāsānañcāyatanasaññāya cittaṃ pakkhandati pasīdati santiṭṭhati adhimuccati* (E^e: *vimuccati*). *so evaṃ pajānāti: ye assu darathā araññasaññaṃ paṭicca te 'dha na santi, ye assu darathā paṭhavīsaññaṃ paṭicca te 'dha na santi, atthi c' evāyaṃ darathamattā yadidaṃ ākāsānañcāyatanasaññaṃ paṭicca ekattan ti. so suññam idaṃ saññāgataṃ araññasaññāyā ti pajānāti, suññam idaṃ saññāgataṃ paṭhavīsaññāyā ti pajānāti, atthi c' ev' idaṃ asuññataṃ yadidaṃ ākāsānañcāyatanasaññaṃ paṭicca ekattan ti. iti yaṃ hi kho tattha na hoti, tena taṃ suññaṃ samanupassati, yaṃ* (E^e: *yam*) *pana tattha avasiṭṭhaṃ hoti, taṃ santam* (E^e and S^e: *santaṃ*) *idam* (B^e and C^e: *idaṃ*) *atthī ti pajānāti. evam pi 'ssa esā, ānanda, yathābhuccā avipallatthā parisuddhā suññatāvakkanti bhavati.*
72. DN 33 at DN III 265,18 and DN 34 at DN III 290,3 (translated by Walshe 1987, 507 and 520), which introduce the set with the qualification that these are *anupubbavihārā*. A parallel to DN 34, T 1.13.240a5, qualifies the same series as 次定 (the Sanskrit fragment parallel has preserved only part of this listing, hence Schlingloff 1962, 22 reconstructs the relevant term *anupūrvavihārāḥ*). Another Pāli occurrence is AN 9.32 at AN IV 410,1 (translated by Bodhi 2012, 1287), in which case a parallel has been preserved in Up 2039 at D 4094 *ju* 70a4 or P 5595 *tu* 78b3, which employs the qualification *mthar gyis gnas pa'i snyoms par 'jug pa*. The different versions thus agree that to proceed through the four absorptions and then the four immaterial spheres, culminating in the attainment of cessation, involves a successive progression or step-by-step sequence.
73. MN 66 at MN I 455,20 (translated by Ñāṇamoli 1995/2005, 558) and MĀ 192 at T 1.26.743b27.
74. AN 3.114 at AN I 267,9 (translated by Bodhi 2012, 347, referred to as discourse 116).
75. SN 15.5 at SN II 181,24 (translated by Bodhi 2000, 654), with parallels in SĀ 949 at T 2.99.242c7, SĀ² 342 at T 2.100.487c26, and EĀ 52.4 at T 2.125.825c12.
76. See in more detail Anālayo 2017a, 109–75 and 2022c, 117–209, as well as 2022f for an exploration of what appears to have motivated the reinterpretation of absorption attainment in scholarly writings.
77. MĀ 190 at T 1.26.737b6: 當數念一無量空處想 (translated by Anālayo 2012a, 28 or 2015, 178) and Skilling 1994, 160,16: *nam mkha' mtha' yas skye mched du 'du shes pa 'am, de las kha cig yid la bya'o.*
78. MN 28 at MN I 190,15 (translated by Ñāṇamoli 1995/2005, 283), with a parallel in

MĀ 30 at T 1.26.466c29 (translated by Bingenheimer, Anālayo, and Bucknell 2013, 232).

79. MN 62 at MN I 424,22: *seyyathā pi, rāhula, ākāso na katthaci patiṭṭhito. evam eva kho tvaṃ, rāhula, ākāsasamaṃ bhāvanaṃ bhāvehi. ākāsasamaṃ* (S^e: *ākāsasamañ*) *hi te, rāhula, bhāvanaṃ bhāvayato uppannā manāpāmanāpā phassā cittaṃ na pariyādāya ṭhassanti*. The situation regarding parallels to this presentation is a bit complex. The parallel to other parts of this discourse, EĀ 17.1, does not cover the four elements and space; see Anālayo 2011a, 348. However, this could be a loss of text due to some shuffling around of material in this discourse collection that appears to have happened in China; see Anālayo 2014/2015, 75–77.
80. MN 152 at MN III 299,6 (translated by Ñāṇamoli 1995/2005, 1148), additionally qualified as "supreme." The parallel SĀ 282 at T 2.99.78b21 instead applies the qualification "noble" to the "cultivation of the faculties," 賢聖修根.
81. On some minor differences between the parallels see Anālayo 2011a, 850–51.
82. MN 21 at MN I 127,30 (translated by Ñāṇamoli 1995/2005, 221) and MĀ 193 at T 1.26.745c11.
83. MN 21 at MN I 128,4: *ākāsasamena cetasā ... viharissāmā* and MĀ 193 at T 1.26.745c25: 心行如虛空.
84. Th 1155 and 1156 (translated by Norman 1969, 106).
85. SN 46.55 at SN V 121,25 (translated by Bodhi 2000, 1611) and AN 5.193 at AN III 230,25 (translated by Bodhi 2012, 807), with a Sanskrit fragment version of the similes in Tripāṭhī 1995, 127–32.
86. Ud 8.1 at Ud 80,15: *appatiṭṭhaṃ* (translated by Ireland 1990, 108).
87. For a survey of references see Anālayo 2023b, 48–49.
88. For a comparative study of a range of parallel versions and a discussion of the significance of this episode see Anālayo 2014a.
89. MN 109 at MN III 17,15 (translated by Ñāṇamoli 1995/2005, 888), SN 22.82 at SN III 101,32 (translated by Bodhi 2000, 925), SĀ 58 at T 2.99.14c11 (translated by Anālayo 2014b, 63) and Up 7006 at D 4094 *nyu* 55a5 or P 5595 *thu* 96b5 (translated by Dhammadinnā 2014, 117) present the first aggregate as depending on the four elements, whereas the next-mentioned three mental aggregates depend on contact, and consciousness depends on name-and-form.
90. Dhp 254: *ākāse va* (not in C^e; E^e: *ca*) *padaṃ n' atthi ... papañcābhiratā pajā, nippapañcā tathāgatā*, with an Indic language parallel in the *Udānavarga* 29.38, Bernhard 1965, 382.
91. MN 121 at MN III 106,11: *puna ca paraṃ, ānanda, bhikkhu amanasikaritvā paṭhavīsaññaṃ* (B^e throughout *pathavī°*; C^e throughout *paṭhavi°*), *amanasikaritvā ākāsānañcāyatanasaññaṃ, viññāṇañcāyatanasaññaṃ paṭicca manasikaroti ekattaṃ. tassa viññāṇañcāyatanasaññāya cittaṃ pakkhandati pasīdati santiṭṭhati adhimuccati* (E^e: *vimuccati*). *so evaṃ pajānāti: ye assu darathā paṭhavīsaññaṃ paṭicca te 'dha na santi, ye assu darathā ākāsānañcāyatanasaññaṃ paṭicca te 'dha na santi, atthi c' evāyaṃ darathamattā yadidaṃ viññāṇañcāyatanasaññaṃ paṭicca ekattan ti. so suññam idaṃ saññāgataṃ paṭhavīsaññāyā ti pajānāti, suññam idaṃ saññāgataṃ ākāsānañcāyatanasaññāyā ti pajānāti, atthi c' ev' idaṃ asuññataṃ yadidaṃ viññāṇañcāyatanasaññaṃ paṭicca ekattan ti. iti yaṃ hi kho tattha na hoti, tena taṃ suññaṃ samanupassati, yaṃ* (E^e: *yam*) *pana tattha avasiṭṭhaṃ hoti, taṃ santam* (E^e and S^e: *santaṃ*) *idam* (B^e and

$\mathrm{C^e}$: *idaṃ) atthī ti pajānāti. evam pi 'ssa esā, ānanda, yathābhuccā* ($\mathrm{E^e}$: *yathābhaccā*) *avipallatthā parisuddhā suññatāvakkanti bhavati.*

92. See, e.g., SN 12.61 at SN II 94,13 (translated by Bodhi 2000, 595) and its parallels in Sanskrit fragments, Chung and Fukita 2020, 113,1, and SĀ 289 at T 2.99.81c7. For discussions of these three terms see also Johansson 1965, Hamilton 1996, 82–114, Somaratne 2005, and Brahmāli 2009, 49–54.
93. See above note 64.
94. The first instance is MN 43 at MN I 292,25 (translated by Ñāṇamoli 1995/2005, 388), which defines consciousness by way of cognizing the three feeling tones; the parallels MĀ 211 at T 1.26.790c6 and Up 9008 at D 4094 *nyu* 81a7 or P 5595 *thu* 127a7 instead speak of cognizing through the six senses. The formulation employed in MN 43 could be a transmission error caused by the same phrasing found in MN 140 at MN III 242,11 (translated by Ñāṇamoli 1995/2005, 1091), a context that does not serve as a general definition of consciousness but much rather describes a specific experience as the outcome of a previous trajectory of meditative cultivation. The second instance is SN 22.79 at SN III 87,17 (translated by Bodhi 2000, 915), which defines consciousness by way of cognizing different flavors, where once again the parallels instead bring in the six senses and their objects; see SĀ 46 at T 2.99.11c9 (translated by Anālayo 2014b, 38) and Up 1014 at D 4094 *ju* 16b4 or P 5595 *tu* 18b1 (translated by Dhammadinnā 2014, 97). The definitions given in MN 43 and SN 22.79 are not wrong as such, since consciousness of course cognizes anything that happens in the mind and therefore also the input provided by feeling tones (MN 43) or by perception (SN 22.79). As noted by Hamilton 1996, 92, consciousness "does not specifically do the discriminating, but, rather, is the awareness by which we experience every stage of the cognitive process, including the process of discriminating." The problem with MN 43 and SN 22.79 is thus only a potential confusion with the role of perception, a problem avoided in the parallels to these two discourses.
95. SN 22.97 at SN III 148,18 (translated by Bodhi 2000, 956) and its parallel EĀ 24.4 at T 2.125.617b12.
96. SN 22.95 at SN III 142,10 (translated by Bodhi 2000, 952), parallel to SĀ 265 at T 2.99.69a7 (translated by Anālayo 2013a, 37), T 1.105.501b9, T 1.106.502a17, and Up 4084 at D 4094 *ju* 240a4 or P 5595 *tu* 274a8 (translated by Dhammadinnā 2013, 77); see also Ñāṇananda 1974/1985, 5–7. According to SĀ 265, T 105, and Up 4084, the magical illusion consists in making various types of military troops appear, such as elephantry, cavalry, chariot troops, or infantry.
97. DN 15 at DN II 56,31 (translated by Walshe 1987, 223), DĀ 13 at T 1.1.61b20 (translated by Anālayo 2018a, 10), MĀ 97 at T 1.26.580a1 (translated by Anālayo 2015, 108), T 1.14.243c2, and T 1.52.845b11.
98. SN 12.2 at SN II 3,34 (translated by Bodhi 2000, 535) and EĀ 49.5 at T 2.125.797b28 (translated by Anālayo 2020a, 1132).
99. Ñāṇavīra 1987/2001, 73 explains: "In any experience (leaving out of account *arūpa*) there is a *phenomenon* that is *present* (i.e. that is cognized). The presence, or cognition, or consciousness, of the phenomenon is *viññāṇa* ... The *designation* of a phenomenon is *nāma* ('name'), which may be seen salso as its *appearance*."
100. SN 12.67 at SN II 114,17 (translated by Bodhi 2000, 608), with parallels in Sanskrit,

Chung and Fukita 2020, 109,1, in SĀ 288 at T 2.99.81b5, and in Up 8005 at D 4094 *nyu* 70a5 or P 5595 *thu* 114b2.

101. Ñāṇananda 1974/1985, 27 reasons: "In this interplay between the two counterparts, consciousness seems to represent actuality while name-and-form stands for potentiality."
102. I am indebted to Ñāṇananda 2016, 17 for the basic idea of this illustration; for a more detailed exploration see Anālayo 2020c.
103. See in more detail Dhammadinnā 2017, 153n9.
104. MN 119 at MN III 93,10 (translated by Ñāṇamoli 1995/2005, 953); the parallel MĀ 81 at T 1.26.555b29 (translated by Anālayo 2017a, 57) only describes a mountain spring that wells up without any inflow from the four directions. Since the idea of an inflow from the four directions is unexpected for a spring, this presentation may be the result of a loss of a reference to a lake that is fed by this spring.
105. Dhp 1: *manopubbaṅgamā dhammā, manoseṭṭhā manomayā*, with Indic language parallels in the Gāndhārī *Dharmapada* 201, Brough 1962/2001, 151, the Patna *Dharmapada* 1, Cone 1989, 104, and the Sanskrit *Udānavarga* 31.23, Bernhard 1965, 415; for a more detailed discussion see Palihawadana 1984, Skilling 2007, and Agostini 2010.
106. In its usage in the early discourses, unification (*ekagga/ekāgra*) of the mind is not confined to absorption attainment; see in more detail Anālayo 2022g.
107. MN 121 at MN III 106,27: *puna ca paraṃ, ānanda, bhikkhu amanasikaritvā ākāsānañcāyatanasaññaṃ, amanasikaritvā viññāṇañcāyatanasaññaṃ, ākiñcaññāyatanasaññaṃ paṭicca manasikaroti ekattaṃ. tassa ākiñcaññāyatanasaññāya cittaṃ pakkhandati pasīdati santiṭṭhati adhimuccati* (E^e: *vimuccati*). *so evaṃ pajānāti: ye assu darathā ākāsānañcāyatanasaññaṃ paṭicca te 'dha na santi, ye assu darathā viññāṇañcāyatanasaññaṃ paṭicca te 'dha na santi, atthi c' evāyaṃ darathamattā yadidaṃ ākiñcaññāyatanasaññaṃ paṭicca ekattan ti. so suññam idaṃ saññāgataṃ ākāsānañcāyatanasaññāyā ti pajānāti, suññam idaṃ saññāgataṃ viññāṇañcāyatanasaññāyā ti pajānāti, atthi c' ev' idaṃ asuññataṃ yadidaṃ ākiñcaññāyatanasaññaṃ paṭicca ekattan ti. iti yaṃ hi kho tattha na hoti, tena taṃ suññaṃ samanupassati, yaṃ pana* (E^e: *yam pi*) *tattha avasiṭṭhaṃ hoti, taṃ santam* (E^e and S^e: *santaṃ*) *idam* (B^e and C^e: *idaṃ*) *atthī ti pajānāti. evam pi 'ssa esā, ānanda, yathābhuccā avipallatthā parisuddhā suññatāvakkanti bhavati.*
108. See Anālayo 2015, 126 and above p. 143.
109. MN 26 at MN I 165,10 (translated by Ñāṇamoli 1995/2005, 258), with parallels in a Sanskrit fragment, folio 331v8, Liu 2010, 155, and MĀ 204 at T 1.26.776c1 (translated by Anālayo 2017c, 44).
110. For a survey of the three approaches see Anālayo 2011a, 615–16.
111. MN 106 at MN II 263,26: *suññam* (E^e: *saññaṃ*) *idaṃ attena vā attaniyena vā ti.*
112. MĀ 75 at T 1.26.542c18: 此世空, 空於神, 神所有, 空有常, 空有恒, 空長存, 空不變易 (translated by Anālayo 2009, 185), Up 4058 at D 4094 *ju* 228b6 or P 5595 *tu* 261a6: *'jig rten ni stong pa'o ... rtag pa dang brtan pa dang g.yung drung dang mi 'gyur ba'i chos can gyis stong zhing bdag dang bdag gi dang bral ba'o* (translated by Anālayo 2009, 186n40).
113. This is the phrase employed by Cousins 2022, 55, who explains (p. 64): "the noun *akiñcanatā* can mean 'renunciation of everything, voluntary poverty' ... I suggest it would be better rendered as the base 'where one has nothing' or the base 'where one

is without possessions' or, perhaps more practically for a translation, the base 'where nothing is owned.'"

114. An example is SN 22.49 at SN III 49,9 (translated by Bodhi 2000, 888), with parallels in a Sanskrit fragment in de La Vallée Poussin 1907, 376 and in SĀ 30 at T 2.99.6b8 (translated by Anālayo 2012b, 49).
115. SN 46.71–73 at SN V 132,18 (translated by Bodhi 2000, 1620), with a parallel in SĀ 747 at T 2.9.198a20; in both versions these three perceptions occur as part of a listing of various perceptions in a discourse repetition series.
116. See in more detail von Rospatt 1995, and on some dimensions of "time" in early Buddhist texts see Anālayo 2019c.
117. EĀ 22.5 at T 2.125.607c15, parallel to AN 3.47 at AN I 152,7 (translated by Bodhi 2012, 246).
118. An example in case is MN 38 at MN I 258,11 (translated by Ñāṇamoli 1995/2005, 350), with parallels in SHT V 1114b1, Sander and Waldschmidt 1985, 109, and MĀ 201 at T 1.26.767a7 (translated by Anālayo 2015, 104).
119. On stream-entry involving such a realization see Anālayo 2023b, 63–64.
120. Sn 231 (translated by Bodhi 2017, 194), with a counterpart in the *Mahāvastu*, Senart 1882, 291,23 (translated by Jones 1949/1973, 243).
121. SN 22.49 at SN III 48,12 (translated by Bodhi 2000, 887), with parallels in a Sanskrit fragment in de La Vallée Poussin 1907, 375 and in SĀ 30 at T 2.99.6a28 (translated by Anālayo 2012b, 48).
122. For an instance where this directly counters the view of a permanent self see MN 22 at MN I 136,14 (translated by Ñāṇamoli 1995/2005, 230), with a parallel in MĀ 200 at T 1.26.764c25.
123. SN 1.25 at SN I 14,14 (translated by Bodhi 2000, 14), with parallels in SĀ 581 at T 2.99.154b27 and SĀ² 166 at T 2.100.435c26.
124. MN 96 at MN II 178,25 (translated by Ñāṇamoli 1995/2005, 787), with a parallel in MĀ 150 at T 1.26.661b1, which contrasts becoming better to remaining the same, rather than to becoming worse. Due to this variation, the two parallels taken together cover the three gradings that correspond to the three modalities of conceit.
125. AN 8.19 at AN IV 203,7 (translated by Bodhi 2012, 1144); see also Ud 5.5 at Ud 56,2 and Vin II 239,32.
126. MĀ 35 at T 1.26.476c11 and EĀ 42.4 at T 2.125.753a28.
127. SN 5.10 at SN I 135,20 (translated by Bodhi 2000, 230), SĀ 1202 at T 2.99.327b9 (translated by Anālayo 2022b, 90), SĀ² 218 at T 2.100.454c29 (translated by Bingenheimer 2011, 171), and Up 9014 at D 4094 *nyu* 82a7 or P 5595 *thu* 128b2 (translated by Dhammadinnā 2020, 9).
128. For a case study of this type of approach in a later Pāli text see Anālayo 2021a.
129. On rebirth and not self see also Anālayo 2019d.
130. See in more detail Anālayo 2017c, 96–114.
131. For an example see Anālayo 2021b, 125.
132. SN 22.83 at SN III 105,14 (translated by Bodhi 2000, 928), with a parallel in SĀ 261 at T 2.99.66a8 (translated by Anālayo 2013a, 16); see in more detail Anālayo 2023b, 147–48.
133. Sn 756: *anattani attamāniṃ* (E^e: *attamānaṃ*; S^e: *attamānī*), *passa lokaṃ sadevakaṃ, niviṭṭhaṃ nāmarūpasmiṃ, idaṃ saccan ti maññati.*

134. MN 121 at MN III 107,26: *puna ca paraṃ, ānanda, bhikkhu amanasikaritvā <viññāṇañcāyatanasaññaṃ>, amanasikaritvā <ākiñcaññāyatanasaññaṃ>, animittaṃ cetosamādhiṃ paṭicca manasikaroti ekattaṃ. tassa animitte cetosamādhimhi cittaṃ pakkhandati pasīdati santiṭṭhati adhimuccati* (E^e: *vimuccati*). *so evaṃ pajānāti: ye assu darathā <viññāṇañcāyatanasaññaṃ> paṭicca te 'dha na santi, ye assu darathā <ākiñcaññāyatanasaññaṃ> paṭicca te 'dha na santi, atthi c' evāyaṃ darathamattā yadidaṃ <animittaṃ cetosamādhiṃ> paṭicca ekattan ti. so suññam idaṃ saññāgataṃ <viññāṇañcāyatanasaññāyā> ti pajānāti, suññam idaṃ saññāgataṃ <ākiñcaññāyatanasaññāyā> ti pajānāti, atthi c' ev' idaṃ asuññataṃ yadidaṃ <animittaṃ cetosamādhiṃ> paṭicca ekattan ti. iti yaṃ hi kho tattha na hoti, tena taṃ suññaṃ samanupassati, yaṃ pana* (E^e: *yam pi*) *tattha avasiṭṭhaṃ hoti, taṃ santam* (E^e and S^e: *santaṃ*) *idam* (B^e and C^e: *idaṃ*) *atthī ti pajānāti. evam pi 'ssa esā, ānanda, yathābhuccā avipallatthā parisuddhā suññatāvakkanti bhavati.*
135. For a more detailed discussion see Anālayo 2015, 134–36.
136. See in more detail Anālayo 2012a, 33–35.
137. Skilling 1994, 172,5: *mtshan ma med pa'i dbyings.*
138. See in more detail Anālayo 2003a.
139. MN 43 at MN I 297,1: *sabbanimittānañ ca amanasikāro, animittāya ca dhātuyā manasikāro*, with a parallel in MĀ 211 at T 1.26.792b13 (translated by Anālayo 2023b, 31).
140. E.g., SN 48.50 at SN V 225,25: *vossaggārammaṇaṃ karitvā labhissati samādhiṃ, labhissati cittassa ekaggataṃ.*
141. See, e.g., MN 107 at MN III 2,14 (translated by Ñāṇamoli 1995/2005, 875), with a parallel in MĀ 144 at T 1.26.652b12. For a more detailed discussion see Anālayo 2023b, 8–11.
142. SN 41.7 at SN IV 297,24 (translated by Bodhi 2000, 1326), with a parallel in SĀ 567 at T 2.99.150a7.
143. Ud 1.10 at Ud 8,4: *tasmātiha te, bāhiya, evaṃ sikkhitabbaṃ: diṭṭhe diṭṭhamattaṃ bhavissati, sute sutamattaṃ bhavissati, mute mutamattaṃ bhavissati, viññāte viññātamattaṃ bhavissatī ti. evañ hi* (C^e: *evaṃ hi*) *te, bāhiya, sikkhitabbaṃ. yato kho te, bāhiya, diṭṭhe diṭṭhamattaṃ bhavissati, sute sutamattaṃ bhavissati, mute mutamattaṃ bhavissati, viññāte viññātamattaṃ bhavissati, tato tvaṃ, bāhiya, na tena; yato tvaṃ, bāhiya, na tena, tato tvaṃ, bāhiya, na tattha; yato tvaṃ, bāhiya, na tattha, tato tvaṃ, bāhiya, nev' idha na huraṃ na ubhayam antarena* (C^e and S^e: *ubhayam antare*). *es' ev' anto dukkhassā ti* (the part between the first and the third *tato tvaṃ* in the above passage is faulty in E^e and S^e and has been restored based on B^e and C^e, whose reading is in line with the corresponding passage of the same instruction in SN 35.95 at SN IV 73,11 in all editions, including E^e and S^e). On my reasons for translating *muta* as "sensed" see Anālayo 2023b, 161n39.
144. MN 22 at MN I 134,30 (translated by Ñāṇamoli 1995/2005, 228) and its parallels MĀ 200 at T 1.26.764b19, EĀ 43.5 at T 2.125.760a13, and Up 8029 at D 4094 *nyu* 74b6 or P 5595 *thu* 119b7.
145. AN 9.37 at AN IV 428,4: *samādhi na cābhinato na cāpanato na ca sasaṅkhāraniggayhavāritagato* (C^e, E^e, and S^e: *sasaṅkhāraniggayhavāritavato*), *vimuttattā ṭhito, ṭhitattā santusito, santusitattā no paritassati*, with a parallel in SĀ 557 at T 2.99.146a16 (translated by Anālayo 2023b, 40). That AN 9.37 would be about signlessness has already been suggested by Harvey 1986, 26; notably a suggestion made without having had

access to the Chinese parallel.

146. *Samāhitā Bhūmiḥ*, Delhey 2009, 186.

147. Dhp 93 (also Th 92): *suññato animitto ca, vimokkho* (E[e]: *vimokho*) *yassa gocaro, ākāse va sakuntānaṃ, padaṃ* (S[e]: *padan*) *tassa durannayaṃ*, with Indic language counterparts in the Patna *Dharmapada* 270, Cone 1989, 267, and the Sanskrit *Udānavarga* 29.31, Bernhard 1965, 381.

148. MN 121 at MN III 108,14: *so evaṃ pajānāti: ayam pi* (S[e]: *hi*) *kho animitto cetosamādhi abhisaṅkhato* (E[e]: *abhisaṃkhato*) *abhisañcetayito* (C[e]: *abhisañcetasiko*). *yaṃ kho pana kiñci abhisaṅkhataṃ* (E[e]: *abhisaṃkhataṃ*) *abhisañcetayitaṃ* (C[e]: *abhisañcetasikaṃ*) *tad aniccaṃ nirodhadhamman ti pajānāti. tassa evaṃ jānato evaṃ passato kāmāsavā pi cittaṃ vimuccati, bhavāsavā pi cittaṃ vimuccati, avijjāsavā pi cittaṃ vimuccati. vimuttasmiṃ vimuttam iti ñāṇaṃ hoti: khīṇā jāti, vusitaṃ brahmacariyaṃ, kataṃ karaṇīyaṃ, nāparaṃ itthattāyā ti pajānāti. so evaṃ pajānāti: ye assu darathā kāmāsavaṃ paṭicca te 'dha na santi, ye assu darathā bhavāsavaṃ paṭicca te 'dha na santi, ye assu darathā avijjāsavaṃ paṭicca te 'dha na santi, atthi c' evāyaṃ darathamattā yadidaṃ imam eva kāyaṃ paṭicca saḷāyatanikaṃ jīvitapaccayā ti. so suññam idaṃ saññāgataṃ kāmāsavenā ti pajānāti, suññam idaṃ saññāgataṃ bhavāsavenā ti pajānāti, suññam idaṃ saññāgataṃ avijjāsavenā ti pajānāti, atthi c' ev' idaṃ asuññataṃ yadidaṃ imam eva kāyaṃ paṭicca saḷāyatanikaṃ jīvitapaccayā ti. iti yaṃ hi kho tattha na hoti, tena taṃ suññaṃ samanupassati, yaṃ pana tattha avasiṭṭhaṃ hoti, taṃ santam* (E[e] and S[e]: *santaṃ*) *idam* (B[e] and C[e]: *idaṃ*) *atthī ti pajānāti. evam assa* (S[e]: *pi 'ssa*) *esā, ānanda, yathābhuccā avipallatthā parisuddhā paramānuttarā suññatāvakkanti bhavati. ye pi* (here and below, E[e] without *pi*) *hi keci, ānanda, atītamaddhānaṃ samaṇā vā brāhmaṇā vā parisuddhaṃ paramānuttaraṃ suññataṃ upasampajja vihariṃsu, sabbe te imaṃ yeva parisuddhaṃ paramānuttaraṃ suññataṃ upasampajja vihariṃsu. ye pi hi keci, ānanda, anāgatamaddhānaṃ samaṇā vā brāhmaṇā vā parisuddhaṃ paramānuttaraṃ suññataṃ upasampajja viharissanti, sabbe te imaṃ yeva parisuddhaṃ paramānuttaraṃ suññataṃ upasampajja viharissanti. ye pi hi keci, ānanda, etarahi samaṇā vā brāhmaṇā vā parisuddhaṃ paramānuttaraṃ suññataṃ upasampajja viharanti, sabbe te imaṃ yeva parisuddhaṃ paramānuttaraṃ suññataṃ upasampajja viharanti. tasmātiha, ānanda, parisuddhaṃ paramānuttaraṃ suññataṃ upasampajja viharissāmā* (E[e]: *viharissāmī*) *ti evañ* (C[e] and E[e]: *evaṃ*) *hi vo, ānanda, sikkhitabban ti.*

149. See in more detail Anālayo 2023b, 68–69.

150. See, e.g., MN 4 at MN I 23,32 (translated by Ñāṇamoli 1995/2005, 107), its parallel EĀ 31.1 at T 2.125.666c22 (translated by Anālayo 2011b, 218–19), and the discussion in Anālayo 2011a, 41.

151. MĀ 190 at T 1.26.737c21 (translated by Anālayo 2012a, 31 or 2015, 180) and Skilling 1994, 178,3.

152. Ps IV 154,16 lists Buddhas, Paccekabuddhas, and disciples of Buddhas.

153. See in more detail Anālayo 2012c, 80–83.

154. MN 149 at MN III 289,7 (translated by Ñāṇamoli 1995/2005, 1138), with parallels in SĀ 305 at T 2.99.87c1 (translated by Anālayo 2022c, 134) and Up 4006 at D 4094 *ju* 205a3 or P 5595 *tu* 234a2; the last differs by assigning right speech to the category of path factors comprised in meditative cultivation, a form of presentation that probably results from a textual error.

155. DN 4 at DN I 124,5 (translated by Walshe 1987, 131) and DĀ 22 at T 1.1.96b18.

156. See in more detail Anālayo 2022c, 117–72 and 2022g.
157. AN 6.60 at AN III 397,11 (translated by Bodhi 2012, 949) and its parallel MĀ 82 at T 1.26.559a21 (translated by Bingenheimer, Anālayo, and Bucknell 2013, 121) depict a monastic gaining signless concentration, followed by subsequently socializing excessively and eventually disrobing. In the ancient setting, taking this step equals not having gained a firm realization.
158. DN 9 at DN I 185,5: *tassa acetayato anabhisaṅkharoto* (E^{e} and S^{e}: *anabhisaṃkharoto*) *tā c' eva saññā nirujjhanti, aññā ca oḷārikā saññā na uppajjanti, so nirodhaṃ phusati*, with parallels in Stuart 2013, 64 and in DĀ 28 at T 1.1.110b29; see also Anālayo 2023b, 175n168.
159. See in more detail Anālayo 2018b, 171–95 and 2019b, 122–54.
160. Yinshun 2017, 76 reasons: "The signless concentration, which does not grasp at or cling to any signs, can be said to be the cultivation [of the awakening factors in a way] that is 'dependent on cessation, inclining towards forsaking.'"
161. SN 2.17 at SN I 54,4: *nāññatra* (E^{e}: *na aññatra*) *sabbanissaggā, sotthiṃ passāmi pāṇinan ti*; the parallels in Enomoto 1989, 26,7 and SĀ 596 at T 2.99.159c29 speak of "liberation" instead of "safety." Another parallel in SĀ^{2} 181 at T 2.100.439a17 proceeds differently.
162. Sn 1094: *akiñcanaṃ anādānaṃ, etaṃ dīpaṃ anāparaṃ, nibbānaṃ iti naṃ brūmi, jarāmaccuparikkhayaṃ*; see also Anālayo 2022a.

References

Agostini, Giulio. 2010. "'Preceded by Thought Are the Dhammas': The Ancient Exegesis on Dhp 1–2." In *Buddhist Asia 2. Papers from the Second Conference of Buddhist Studies Held in Naples in June 2004*, edited by Giacomella Orofino and Silvio Vita, 1–34. Kyoto: Italian School of East Asian Studies.

Anālayo, Bhikkhu. 2003a. "Nimitta." In *Encyclopaedia of Buddhism, Volume 7*, edited by W. G. Weeraratne, 177–79. Sri Lanka: Department of Buddhist Affairs.

———. 2003b. *Satipaṭṭhāna: The Direct Path to Realization*. Birmingham: Windhorse Publications.

———. 2008. "The Sixfold Purity of an Arahant According to the *Chabbisodhana-sutta* and Its Parallel." *Journal of Buddhist Ethics*, 15: 241–77.

———. 2009. "The *Āneñjasappāya-sutta* and Its Parallels on Imperturbability and on the Contribution of Insight to the Development of Tranquillity." *Buddhist Studies Review*, 26.2: 177–95.

———. 2011a. *A Comparative Study of the Majjhima-nikāya*. Taipei: Dharma Drum Publishing Corporation.

———. 2011b. "Living in Seclusion and Facing Fear: The Ekottarika-āgama Counterpart to the Bhayabherava-sutta." In *Buddhism as a Stronghold of Free Thinking? Social, Ethical and Philosophical Dimensions of Buddhism*, edited by Siegfried C. A. Fay and Ilse Maria Bruckner, 203–31. Germany, Nuesttal: Edition Ubuntu.

———. 2011c. "Right View and the Scheme of the Four Truths in Early Buddhism: The Saṃyukta-āgama Parallel to the Sammādiṭṭhi-sutta and the Simile of the Four Skills of a Physician." *Canadian Journal of Buddhist Studies*, 7: 11–44.

———. 2012a. "A Gradual Entry into Emptiness: Depicted in the Early Buddhist Discourses." *Thai International Journal of Buddhist Studies*, 3: 25–56.

———. 2012b. "On the Five Aggregates (1): A Translation of *Saṃyukta-āgama* Discourses 1 to 32." *Dharma Drum Journal of Buddhist Studies*, 11: 1–61.

———. 2012c. "Purification in Early Buddhist Discourse and Buddhist Ethics." *Bukkyō Kenkyū*, 40: 67–97.

———. 2013a. "On the Five Aggregates (2): A Translation of *Saṃyukta-āgama* Discourses 256 to 272." *Dharma Drum Journal of Buddhist Studies*, 12: 1–69.

———. 2013b. *Perspectives on Satipaṭṭhāna*. Cambridge: Windhorse Publications.

———. 2014a. "The Buddha's Last Meditation in the *Dīrgha-āgama*." *Indian International Journal of Buddhist Studies*, 15: 1–43.

———. 2014b. "On the Five Aggregates (4): A Translation of *Saṃyukta-āgama* Discourses 33 to 58." *Dharma Drum Journal of Buddhist Studies*, 14: 1–71.

———. 2014/2015. "Discourse Merger in the *Ekottarika-āgama* (2): The Parallels to the *Kakacūpama-sutta* and the *Alagaddūpama-sutta*." *Journal of Buddhist Studies*, 12: 63–90.

———. 2015. *Compassion and Emptiness in Early Buddhist Meditation*. Cambridge: Windhorse Publications.

———. 2016a. "The Gradual Path of Training in the *Dīrgha-āgama*, From Sense-Restraint to Imperturbability." *Indian International Journal of Buddhist Studies*, 17: 1–24.

———. 2016b. *Mindfully Facing Disease and Death: Compassionate Advice from Early Buddhist Texts*. Cambridge: Windhorse Publications.

———. 2017a. *Early Buddhist Meditation Studies*. Barre, MA: Barre Center for Buddhist Studies.

———. 2017b. "How Compassion Became Painful." *Journal of Buddhist Studies* 14: 85–113.

———. 2017c. *A Meditator's Life of the Buddha: Based on the Early Discourses*. Cambridge: Windhorse Publications.

———. 2018a. *Rebirth in Early Buddhism and Current Research.* Somerville, MA: Wisdom Publications.

———. 2018b. *Satipaṭṭhāna Meditation: A Practice Guide.* Cambridge: Windhorse Publications.

———. 2019a. *Mindfully Facing Climate Change.* Barre, MA: Barre Center for Buddhist Studies.

———. 2019b. *Mindfulness of Breathing: A Practice Guide and Translations.* Cambridge: Windhorse Publications.

———. 2019c. "On Time." *Insight Journal*, 45: 11–20.

———. 2019d. "Rebirth and the West." *Insight Journal*, 45: 55–64.

———. 2020a. "Attention and Mindfulness." *Mindfulness*, 11.5: 1131–38.

———. 2020b. "Buddhist Antecedents to the Body Scan Meditation." *Mindfulness*, 11.1: 194–202.

———. 2020c. "The Five 'Fingers' of Name." *Insight Journal*, 46: 27–36.

———. 2021a. "The Opening Debate in the *Milindapañha*." *Sri Lanka International Journal of Buddhist Studies*, 7.2: 15–27.

———. 2021b. *Superiority Conceit in Buddhist Traditions: A Historical Perspective.* Somerville, MA: Wisdom Publications.

———. 2022a. "Being Mindful of What Is Absent." *Mindfulness*, 13.7: 1671–78.

———. 2022b. *Daughters of the Buddha: Teachings by Ancient Indian Women.* Somerville, MA: Wisdom Publications.

———. 2022c. *Developments in Buddhist Meditation Traditions: The Interplay Between Theory and Practice.* Barre, MA: Barre Center for Buddhist Studies.

———. 2022d. *Early Buddhist Oral Tradition: Textual Formation and Transmission.* Somerville, MA: Wisdom Publications.

———. 2022e. "Education and Mindfulness: An Early Buddhist Contribution to the Ongoing Dialog." *Mindfulness*, 13.10: 2413–19.

———. 2022f. "Reinterpreting Absorption: A Critical Examination of a Trend in Buddhist Studies." *Journal of Buddhist Studies*, 19: 121–49.

———. 2022g. "The Role of Absorption for Entering the Stream." *Journal of Buddhist Studies*, 19: 1–26.

———. 2023a. "Early Buddhism." *Insight Journal*, 49: 23–34.

———. 2023b. *The Signless and the Deathless: On the Realization of Nirvana*. Somerville, MA: Wisdom Publications.

Anālayo, Bhikkhu and Roderick S. Bucknell. 2020. *The Madhyama Āgama (Middle Length Discourses), Volume II*. Berkeley, CA: Numata Center for Buddhist Translation and Research.

Bendall, Cecil. 1902/1970. *Çikshāsamuccaya: A Compendium of Buddhistic Teaching Compiled by Çāntideva, Chiefly from Earlier Mahāyāna-Sūtras*. Osnabrück: Biblio Verlag.

Bendall, Cecil and W. H. D. Rouse. 1922/1990. *Śikṣā Samuccaya: A Compendium of Buddhist Doctrine, Compiled by Śāntideva, Chiefly from Earlier Mahāyāna-Sūtras, Translated from the Sanskrit*. Delhi: Motilal Banarsidass.

Bernhard, Franz. 1965. *Udānavarga, Band 1*. Göttingen: Vandenhoeck & Ruprecht.

Bingenheimer, Marcus. 2011. *Studies in Āgama Literature: With Special Reference to the Shorter Chinese Saṃyuktāgama*. Taipei: Shin Weng Feng Print Co.

Bingenheimer, Marcus, Bhikkhu Anālayo, and Roderick S. Bucknell. 2013. *The Madhyama Āgama (Middle Length Discourses), Volume I*. Berkeley, CA: Numata Center for Buddhist Translation and Research.

Bodhi, Bhikkhu. 2000. *The Connected Discourses of the Buddha: A New Translation of the Saṃyutta Nikāya*. Somerville, MA: Wisdom Publications.

———. 2012. *The Numerical Discourses of the Buddha: A Translation of the Aṅguttara Nikāya*. Somerville, MA: Wisdom Publications.

———. 2017. *The Suttanipāta: An Ancient Collection of the Buddha's Discourses, Together with Its Commentaries—Paramatthajotikā II and Excerpts from the Niddesa*. Somerville, MA: Wisdom Publications.

Brahmāli, Bhikkhu. 2009: "What the Nikāyas Say and Do Not Say about Nibbāna." *Buddhist Studies Review*, 26.1: 33–66.

Brough, John. 1962/2001. *The Gāndhārī Dharmapada: Edited with an Introduction and Commentary*. Delhi: Motilal Banarsidass.

Chalmers, Robert. 1927. *Further Dialogues of the Buddha: Translated from the Pali of the Majjhima Nikāya, Volume II*. London: Oxford University Press.

Ñāṇavīra Thera. 1987/2001. *Clearing the Path: Writings of Ñāṇavīra Thera (1960–1965), Volume I, Notes on Dhamma.* Dehiwala, Sri Lanka: Buddhist Cultural Centre.

Norman, K. R. 1969. *The Elders' Verses I: Theragāthā, Translated with an Introduction and Notes.* London: Pali Text Society.

Palihawadana, Mahinda. 1984. "Dhammapada 1 and 2 and Their Commentaries." In *Buddhist Studies in Honor of Hammalava Saddhatissa*, edited by Gatare Dhammapāla, Richard Gombrich, and K. R. Norman, 189–202. Nugegoda, Sri Lanka: University of Jayewardenepura.

Plofker, Kim. 2009. *Mathematics in India.* Princeton, NJ: Princeton University Press.

Pradhan, P. 1967. *Abhidharmakośabhāṣya of Vasubandhu.* Patna: Kashi Prasad Jayaswal Research Institute.

Pruden, Leo M. 1990. *Abhidharmakośabhāṣyam by Louis de la Vallée Poussin, Volume IV.* Berkeley, CA: Asian Humanity Press.

Rossi, Paola M. 2010. "Forest of Desires and Desire of Forests: A Way to the Buddhist Ethics." *Res Antiquitatis, Journal of Ancient History*, 1: 181–214.

Sander, Lore and Ernst Waldschmidt. 1985. *Sanskrithandschriften aus den Turfanfunden, Teil 5.* Stuttgart: Franz Steiner.

Schlingloff, Dieter. 1962. *Dogmatische Begriffsreihen im älteren Buddhismus. Ia: Daśottarasūtra IX–X.* Berlin: Akademie Verlag.

Schmithausen, Lambert. 1981. "On Some Aspects of Descriptions or Theories of 'Liberating Insight' and 'Enlightenment' in Early Buddhism." In *Studien zum Jainismus und Buddhismus, Gedenkschrift für Ludwig Alsdorf*, edited by Klaus Bruhn and Albert Wezler, 199–250. Wiesbaden: Franz Steiner.

Senart, Émile. 1882. *Le Mahāvastu: Texte sanscrit publié pour la première fois et accompagné d'introductions et d'un commentaire, Tome premier.* Paris: Imprimerie Nationale.

Skilling, Peter. 1994. *Mahāsūtras: Great Discourses of the Buddha, Volume I: Texts.* Oxford: Pali Text Society.

———. 1997. *Mahāsūtras: Great Discourses of the Buddha, Volume II.* Oxford: Pali Text Society.

———. 2007. "'Dhammas Are as Swift as Thought ...' A Note on

Dhammapada 1 and 2 and Their Parallels." *Journal of the Centre for Buddhist Studies*, 5: 23–50.

Soma Thera. 1941/1981. *The Way of Mindfulness: The Satipaṭṭhāna Sutta Commentary*. Kandy: Buddhist Publication Society.

Somaratne, G. A. 2005. "Citta, Manas and Viññāṇa: Aspects of Mind as Presented in Early Buddhist Pali Discourses." In *Dhamma-Vinaya, Essays in Honour of Venerable Professor Dhammavihari (Jotiya Dhirasekera)*, edited by Asaṅga Tilakaratne, Endo Tochiichi, and G. A. Somaratne, 169–202. Colombo: Sri Lanka Association for Buddhist Studies.

Śrāvakabhūmi Study Group. 1998. *Śrāvakabhūmi: Revised Sanskrit Text and Japanese Translation, The First Chapter*. Tokyo: Sankibo.

Stache-Rosen, Valentina. 1968. *Dogmatische Begriffsreihen im älteren Buddhismus II: Das Saṅgītisūtra und sein Kommentar Saṅgītiparyāya*. Berlin: Akademie Verlag.

Stuart, Daniel M. 2013. *Thinking about Cessation: The Pṛṣṭhapālasūtra of the Dīrghāgama in Context*. Wien: Arbeitskreis für Tibetische und Buddhistische Studien, Universität Wien.

Treleaven, David A. 2018. *Trauma-Sensitive Mindfulness: Practices for Safe and Transformative Healing*. New York: W. W. Norton & Company.

Tripāṭhī, Chandrabhal. 1995. *Ekottarāgama-Fragmente der Gilgit-Handschrift*. Reinbek: Verlag für Orientalistische Fachpublikationen.

Visigalli, Paolo. 2019. "Chartering 'Wilderness' (araṇya) in Brahmanical and Buddhist Texts." *Indo-Iranian Journal*, 62: 162–89.

von Rospatt, Alexander. 1995. *The Buddhist Doctrine of Momentariness: A Survey of the Origins and Early Phase of This Doctrine up to Vasubandhu*. Stuttgart: Franz Steiner Verlag.

Waldschmidt, Ernst. 1951. *Das Mahāparinirvāṇasūtra: Text in Sanskrit und Tibetisch, verglichen mit dem Pāli nebst einer Übersetzung der chinesischen Entsprechung im Vinaya der Mūlasarvāstivādins, auf Grund von Turfan-Handschriften herausgegeben und bearbeitet, Teil II: Textbearbeitung*. Berlin: Akademie Verlag.

Walshe, Maurice. 1987. *Thus Have I Heard: The Long Discourses of the Buddha*. London: Wisdom Publications.

Wayman, Alex. 1997. *Untying the Knots in Buddhism: Selected Essays*. Delhi: Motilal Banarsidass Publishers.

Yinshun, Venerable. 2017. *An Investigation into Emptiness, Parts One & Two*. Translated by Shi Huifeng. Towaco, NJ: Noble Path Buddhist Education Fellowship.

Index

Q

R

S

T

U

About the Author

BHIKKHU ANĀLAYO is a scholar of early Buddhism and a meditation teacher. He completed his PhD research on the *Satipaṭṭhāna-sutta* at the University of Peradeniya, Sri Lanka, in 2000 and his habilitation research with a comparative study of the *Majjhimanikāya* in the light of its Chinese, Sanskrit, and Tibetan parallels at the University of Marburg, Germany, in 2007. His over five hundred publications are for the most part based on comparative studies, with a special interest in topics related to meditation and the role of women in Buddhism.

What to Read Next from Wisdom Publications

The Signless and the Deathless
On the Realization of Nirvana
Bhikkhu Anālayo

"Venerable Anālayo skillfully illuminates how some of the earliest Buddhist texts provide a systematic path for engaging with and experiencing the world in its pure essence, free from the defilements that cause so much suffering. He then takes us one step further to show how this clear perception, once applied and stable, recognizes Nirvana for what it truly is: empty or deathless. An essential read for students of the Buddhadharma." —Yongey Mingyur Rinpoche

Daughters of the Buddha
Teachings by Ancient Indian Women
Bhikkhu Anālayo

"The aspirations of women in ancient India and those of us in the present may not be the same, but the courage and struggle for liberation highlighted in their stories will no doubt provide a main source of inspiration to many struggling women in today's world." —Professor Hiroko Kawanami, author of *The Culture of Giving in Myanmar*

Early Buddhist Oral Tradition
Textual Formation and Transmission
Bhikkhu Anālayo

In-depth but still accessible, *Early Buddhist Oral Tradition* is an engrossing and enlightening inquiry into the early Buddhist oral tradition.

Rebirth in Early Buddhism and Current Research
Bhikkhu Anālayo

"Bhikkhu Anālayo offers a detailed study of the much-debated Buddhist doctrine of rebirth and a survey of relevant evidence. He also investigates the Pāli chantings of Dhammaruwan, who at a very young age would spontaneously chant ancient and complex Buddhist suttas. I first met Dhammaruwan when he was seven years old, when my teacher, Anagarika Munindraji, and I visited him and his family in Sri Lanka. *Rebirth in Early Buddhism and Current Research* illuminates a complex topic with great clarity and understanding." —Joseph Goldstein, author of *Mindfulness: A Practical Guide to Awakening*

Superiority Conceit in Buddhist Traditions
A Historical Perspective
Bhikkhu Anālayo

"This book is a courageous call for integrity and self-reflection. Bhikkhu Anālayo argues that if Buddhism is to engage the modern world with any enduring success, it must abandon its own conceit and reckon with its internal prejudices. This book is a much-needed contribution that will help reshape the direction of the field." —Vanessa Sasson, professor, Marianopolis College

About Wisdom Publications

Wisdom Publications is the leading publisher of classic and contemporary Buddhist books and practical works on mindfulness. To learn more about us or to explore our other books, please visit our website at wisdomexperience.org or contact us at the address below.

Wisdom Publications
132 Perry Street
New York, NY 10014 USA

We are a 501(c)(3) organization, and donations in support of our mission are tax deductible.

Wisdom Publications is affiliated with the Foundation for the Preservation of the Mahayana Tradition (FPMT).